Kindergarten

Hooked on Phonics®

Beginning Words

Designed and illustrated by
Big Yellow Taxi, Inc.

The Alphabet

Say the name of each thing out loud.
Listen for the sound of the letter in the word.

a

g

b

h

c

i

d

j

e

k

f

l

Help Pig Wig

Draw a path through the **ig** words to get Pig Wig to the park.
Draw a path through the **id** words to get Pig Wig to the store.

rap	rig	fat	did	bid	nag
mat	wig	zig	lid	hid	lap
van	big	dig	tap	rid	fan

Hooked on Kindergarten *Super Workbook*

it and in

Write the letter "i" on each line.
Say each word out loud.

s_i_t

h_t

f_n

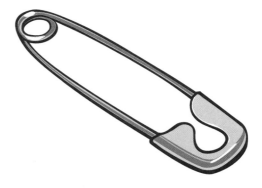

p_n

In the Bin

Help Pig Wig clean up.
Draw a line from each **in** word to the **in** bin.
Draw a line from each **it** word to the **it** bin.

fin

tin

sit

pin

fit

bit

hit

win

in

it

13

Word Match

Draw a line from each word on the left to a word on the right that ends with the same sound.

kid

dig

hit

lid

pig

sit

14

The Big Pit

Pig Wig can dig.

"Pig Wig!
Did you dig a big pit?"

"I did it."

The big pit is a big hit!

Shopping for Words

Look around your home for things with **at**, **an**, **ap**, and **ag** sounds.

Put them in a bag. Use the shopping list to help you.

Take each thing out of the bag. Say its name out loud.

List:
can
cap
hat
mat
map
pan
rag

Note to Parents
You may find other things with the short **a** sound to add to your bag. After unpacking the bag, make a tag for each item. Your child may wish to write the word on his own, or he can trace yours. Be sure to point out each ending sound.

Tongue Twisters

Read one of the silly sentences below.

Say it fast as many times as you can. Then try another tongue twister!

The big kid hid in the big bin.

The pig in a wig wins a pin.

Can a big rig dig a big pit?

The fish with the fin sits in a pit.

Note to Parents
These tongue twisters all contain three-letter words with the short i sound. See if you and your child can make up more tongue twisters together.

Hooked on Kindergarten *Super Workbook*

ox and ot

Write the letter "o" on each line.
Say each word out loud.

f_o_x

b_x

h_t

p_t

Hot Pot

Circle the things with the **ot** sound.
Draw an X on the things with the **ox** sound.

cap

bag

ox

pot

Pop Fox

box

dot

Hooked on Kindergarten *Super Workbook*

Write the letter "o" on each line.
Say each word out loud.

m _o_ p

h _ p

d _ g

l _ g

Pop Fox Hops

Help Pop Fox cross the pond.
Color each log with an **op** or **og** word on it to make a path.

pop

hog

fox

dog

dot

box

fog

ox

mop

not

top

Hooked on Kindergarten *Super Workbook*

Word Match

Draw a line from each thing to the matching word.

fox

dog

pot

mop

Pop Fox Got Hot

Pop Fox can jog.

Pop Fox can hop.

Pop Fox can mop.

Pop Fox got hot.

Hooked on Kindergarten *Super Workbook*

Write the letter "u" on each line.
Say each word out loud.

b_u_g

h_g

s_n

r_n

Help Dog Bug

Draw a path through the **ug** words to get
Dog Bug to the pond.
Draw a path through the **un** words to get
Dog Bug to the flowers.

rap	bug	fat	did	sun	nag
tug	rug	mat	run	fun	lap
jug	hug	van	bun	pun	fan

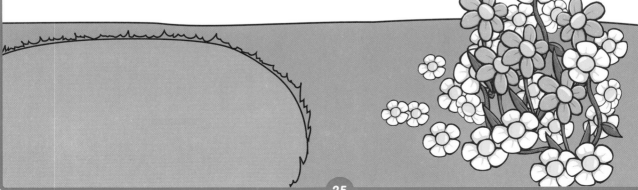

25

ub and ut

Write the letter "u" on each line.
Say each word out loud.

t_u_b

s_b

c_t

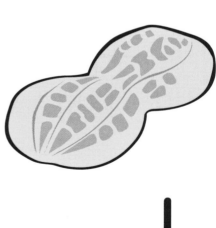

n_t

Word Scramble

Unscramble the letters into words.
Write the words on the lines.

ubs____   tbu____

tuc____   utn____

Word Match

Draw a line from each word on the left to a word on the right that ends with the same sound.

sun

nut

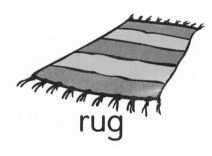

bug

rug

tub

run

cut

cub

28

Where Is Dog Bug?

Where is Dog Bug?
On the rug?

Where is Dog Bug?
In the tub?

Here is Dog Bug!
In the jug.

That was fun!

29

Hot Potato

This is a game for two or more players.

How to play:

Sit in a circle and pass a potato.

When a player gets the "hot potato," it's his turn.

The player quickly says a word with an **ot** sound, such as **hot**.

Then he passes the potato to the next player.

Note to Parents
Use this fun and fast-paced game to review the short **o** sounds your child has practiced in this workbook—three-letter words ending in **ox**, **ot**, **op**, and **og**. Have another player outside the circle make a written list of the words used during the game. Ask your child to read the list out loud when the game is over.

Acting Up!

This is a game for two or more players.

How to play:

Write the words in the box on index cards.

Put the cards into a hat or bowl.

The first player chooses a card and acts out the word on the card.

The other players try to guess the word.

Take turns until all of the cards have been acted out.

bug
hug
run
rub
cut
nut
sun

Note to Parents
Act out three-letter words with the short **u** sound. If needed, whisper the word to your child so he may act it out for others to guess.

ed and et

Write the letter "e" on each line.
Say each word out loud.

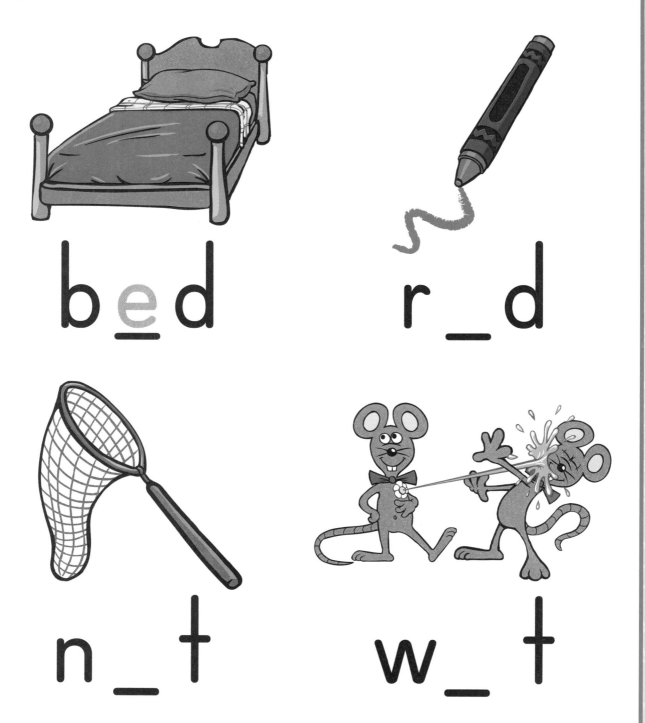

b_e_d

r_d

n_t

w_t

The Pet

Draw a path through the **ed** and **et** words to help Pig Wig get her pet to the vet.

cat	lap	bed	bid	cat	lap
fun	not	set	sit	fun	not
cat	red	wet			
sit	fed	get			

Hooked on Kindergarten *Super Workbook*

Write the letter "e" on each line.
Say each word out loud.

p _e_ n

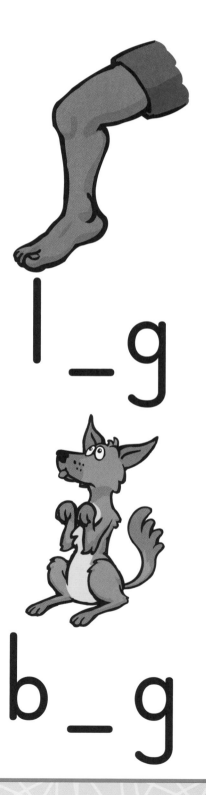

l _ g

t _ n

b _ g

Happy Hens

Color each hen on an **en** word red.
Color each hen on an **eg** word yellow.

hen

beg

leg

men

pen

peg

Word Match

Draw a line from each thing to the matching word.

bed

ten

wet

leg

Ten Red Hens

Ten red hens went in a pen.

Ten red hens get fed.

Ten red hens get wet.

Ten red hens went to bed.

Hooked on Kindergarten *Super Workbook*

Look Ahead

This is a game for two or more players.

How to play:

The first player looks around for something red.

When he has found it, he says to the other players, "Look ahead for something red."

The other players try to guess what the player has found.

Then take turns spotting more red things!

Note to Parents
This take on the classic spying game lets you and your child have fun with the word *red*. You might want to extend this game to other three-letter words with the short **e** sound. See if your child can find a bed, a leg, a pet, or something wet.

Animal Book

Make your own book of animals!

Draw a picture of each animal on the list.

Write the animal's name under your drawing.

bat

bug

cat

hen

rat

dog

fox

pig

Note to Parents
After your child has drawn each animal on a separate
sheet of paper, help him make a cover for the book. Help
him think of a title and a picture for the cover and be sure
to include the author's name! Then staple all of the pages
together to make a book.

Hooked on Kindergarten *Super Workbook*

Write an "e" on each line.
Say each word out loud.

rak_e_

vas_

wav_

cav_

The Lake

Circle all of the words with the long **a** sound as in **lake**.

cake bat

late same

man

rag map

made

Hooked on Kindergarten *Super Workbook*

MEGA GAME

Dog Bug's Words

Dog Bug is thinking of some words.
Say the name of each thing out loud.
Color the things that have the long a sound
as in made.

42

The Same Cake

Pig Wig bakes a cake.

Pop Fox bakes a cake.

Look!
The cakes are the same!

Now there is
more cake to share.

Write an "e" on each line.
Say each word out loud.

bik<u>e</u>

kit_

tir_

fir_

I Find

Circle the things with the long **i** sound as in **wire**.

kite

wire

ball

tire

bike

pail

45

Circle the Picture

Say the name of each thing out loud.
Circle the thing in each row with the
long **i** sound as in **mine**.

A Bike Ride

"Would you like to go on a bike ride?"

"I like riding bikes."

"My tire!"

"A hike is fine, too!"

Hooked on Kindergarten *Super Workbook*

A Race!

Write the words in the box on index cards.

Put four cards in one spot. Put four cards in another spot.

Start in one spot. Pick a card. Read the word out loud.
Run to the next spot. Pick a card. Read the word out loud.

Go back and forth until you read all of the words out loud.

How fast can you do it?

cake
lake
came
same
cane
made
race
wave

Note to Parents
Help your child choose the two spots to place the cards.
Two chairs a short distance apart would be ideal. You can
use a stopwatch or clock to time him.

Storyteller

Write each word in the box on a card.

Put the cards in a bag. Pick three cards.

Make up a story using the three words.

bike

fine

fire

kite

mile

pile

time

tire

Note to Parents
As your child masters reading the words on the cards, add new cards of simple long-vowel words to your collection.

49

o as in rope

Write an "e" on each line.
Say each word out loud.

rop_e_

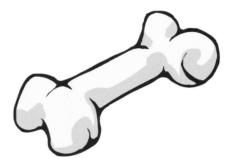

bon_

nos_

ros_

The Rose Garden

Color each rose that has a word with the long o sound as in rose.

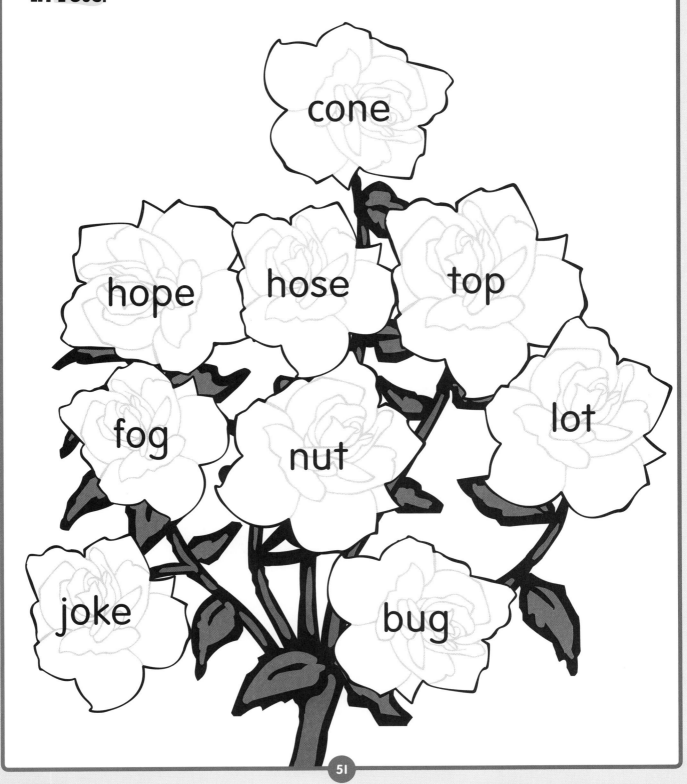

cone

hope

hose

top

fog

nut

lot

joke

bug

51

Color the Bones

Color each bone that has a word with the long **o** sound as in **bone**.

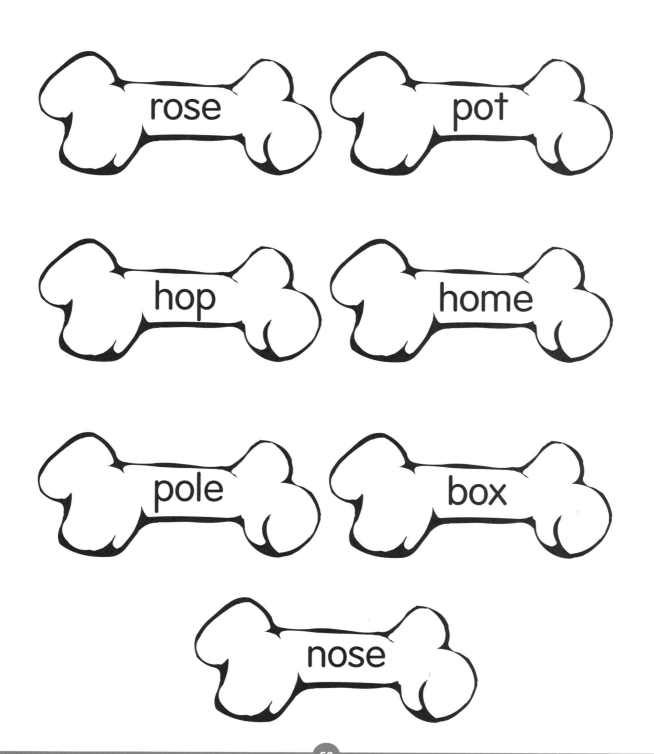

rose

pot

hop

home

pole

box

nose

Oh, Rats!

A pole.

A rope.

A note.

A hose. Oh no!

Hooked on Kindergarten *Super Workbook*

u as in cute

Write an "e" on each line.
Say each word out loud.

cub**e**

tub_

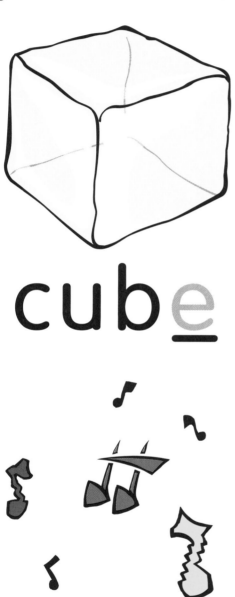

tun_

mul_

Color the Cubes

Color each cube that has a word with the long **u** sound as in **tune**.

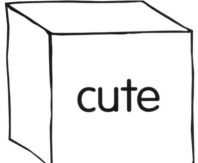

cute

tube

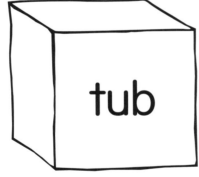

tub

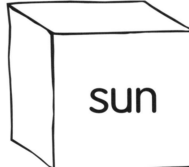

sun

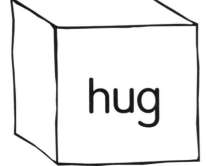

hug

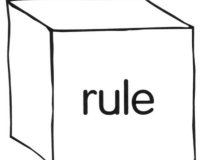

rule

Hooked on Kindergarten *Super Workbook*

Get the Mule!

Help Pop Fox get to the mule.
Draw a path through the words with the long **u** sound as in **mule**.

bun	cut	hut	rule	tune
cup				
pup		cute	mule	
	fun	tube	bun	fun
tune	duke	pup		
cup	cure	dune		

Hooked on Kindergarten *Super Workbook*

At the Play Place

A tube.

A cube.

A tune.

How cute!

Home, Sweet Home

Go on a scavenger hunt in your home.

See how many things on the list you can find.

rope

bone

nose

cone

hose

pole

note

Note to Parents
Look for words with the long **o** sound made with silent "e." If you have trouble finding the items, sit down with your child and draw pictures of them instead.

A Silly Tune

Read the silly poem.

Can you make up a tune to go with the words?

"The Duke and His Mule"

The duke has a mule!
The duke has a mule!
The mule is so big.
The mule is so huge!
People can be rude.
They say, "Who's pulling whom?"
The mule has a duke!
The mule has a duke!

Note to Parents
The words in this silly song are words with the long **u** sound made with silent "e." Read the poem out loud to your child several times. If your child has trouble making up a tune, use the tune of a familiar song.

Hooked on Kindergarten *Super Workbook*

A Magic Trick

How can you turn a can into a cane? Use silent "e"!
Turn the words on the next page into new words.
Cut on the dotted lines.
Fold the flap back on the red line. Presto!
Can you say the new word?

cub

can

cap

pin

tub

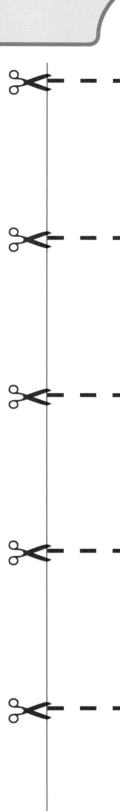

Hooked on Kindergarten *Super Workbook*

e

e

e

e

e

More Magic

Turn these words into new words.
Just add silent "e"!

hide

man _

hop _

mat _

tot _

cut _

Hooked on Kindergarten *Super Workbook*

I did it!

Congratulations!

_____

_ _

_____

has successfully completed this workbook.

Kindergarten
Hooked on Phonics®

Rhyming Words and More

Say the Sound

Say the name of each thing out loud.
Listen for the sound of the letter in the word.

a		g	
b		h	
c		i	
d		j	
e		k	
f		l	

m		t	
n		u	
o		v	
p		w	
q		x	
r		y	
s		z	

Sound Match

Help Pop Fox clean up the mess.
Say the name of each thing out loud.
Draw a line to match each thing to the letter that begins its name.

Hooked on Kindergarten *Super Workbook*

X Marks the Spot

I did it!

Look at the things in each row.
Draw an X on the thing that does not begin
with the sound of the letter on the left.

m

n

p

b

69

Animal Match

Say the name of each animal out loud.
Draw a line to match each animal to the letter that begins its name.

s

d

c

w

Circle It!

I did it!

Look at the things in each row.
Circle the thing that begins with the sound of
the letter on the left.

h

w

s

d

Hooked on Kindergarten *Super Workbook*

Name Game

Say the name of each thing out loud.
Circle the letter that begins its name.

f   s

b   g

f   j

r   g

72

Oh, Brother!

Look at the letter the first Ratini is holding.
Circle the brother with the thing that begins with the
sound of the letter.

Hooked on Kindergarten *Super Workbook*

Letter Match

Say the name of each thing out loud.
Draw a line to match each thing to the letter that begins its name.

g

c

f

h

k

d

s

p

w

74

Circle Time

Say the name of each thing out loud.
Circle the letter that begins its name.

g l   m b   t n

j v   f q   z c

b c   h u   p b

Hooked on Kindergarten *Super Workbook*

The Sound of Letters

Say the name of each thing out loud.
Circle the letter that begins its name.

 r   v

 l   t

 r   b

 y   x

 z   v

Sound Roundup

Say the name of each thing out loud.
Circle the two things in each row that begin with the same sound.

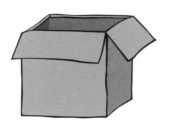  

Hooked on Kindergarten *Super Workbook*

Vowel Hunt

Say the name of each thing out loud.
Circle the letter that begins its name.

i a

i e

a o

u i

o e

Color It!

Color the thing that has a short **a** sound as in **can**.

Color the thing that has a short **i** sound as in **pig**.

Color the thing that has a short **o** sound as in **fox**.

Color the thing that has a short **u** sound as in **bus**.

Color the thing that has a short **e** sound as in **bed**.

Hooked on Kindergarten *Super Workbook*

MEGA GAME

Letter Blocks

Say the name of each thing out loud.
Draw a line to match each thing to the letter that begins its name.

r

t

v

q

x

y

z

Hooked on Kindergarten *Super Workbook*

Circle Time

Say the name of each thing out loud.
Circle the letter that begins its name.

r   s

t   b

o   a

y   z

z   c

a   o

v   i

h   u

q   e

Hooked on Kindergarten *Super Workbook*

Sound Walk

This is a game for two or more players.

How to play:

1. One player calls out a letter sound.

2. The next player looks around and names a thing that begins with that same sound.

3. Players take turns naming things that begin with the letter sound. When a player can't find anything else to name, another player calls out a different letter sound.

4. Use the chart on the next page to write down something you found that begins with each letter sound.

Note to Parents
Try to get your child thinking and talking about the sounds of letters by playing this game. You can call out things that you really see, or you can be imaginative and make things up. Encourage your child to keep trying if he has a difficult time isolating the beginning letter sound of a word.

a	n
b	o
c	p
d	q
e	r
f	s
g	t
h	u
i	v
j	w
k	x
l	y
m	z

Vowel Hunt

Help the Ratinis pack their van.
Circle the things that rhyme with van.

Hooked on Kindergarten *Super Workbook*

Follow the Rhymes

Help Hip-O find his pail.
Draw a path through the things that rhyme with **pail**.

START

Hooked on Kindergarten *Super Workbook*

Pick-up Sticks

Circle the things that rhyme with sticks.

Hooked on Kindergarten *Super Workbook*

I Rhyme

Look at the things in each row.
Say their names out loud.
Circle the two things that rhyme.

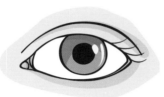  

Hooked on Kindergarten *Super Workbook*

Let's Rhyme

Circle the things that rhyme with fox.

The Boat Floats

Help Pop Fox get to the island.
Draw a path through the things that rhyme with float.

START

89

Hooked on Kindergarten *Super Workbook*

That Cat

Here's a pretty kitty.

It skips and flips.

The ice cream drips.

It gives Hip-O
a quick lick.

Hops and Flops

The rain drops.

Dog Bug hops.

Dog Bug flops.

The rain stops!

Snug Hug

Circle the things that rhyme with snug.

Rhymes for You

Look at the things in each row.
Say their names out loud.
Circle the two things that rhyme.

 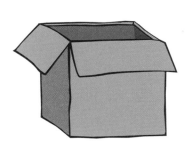 

Get the Net

Draw lines to match Hip-O to the things that rhyme with net.

Make a Rhyme

Circle the picture to complete each rhyme.

If I were a ,

I would wear a _____ .

I would hide in a

and stay close to the _____ .

I'd live in your

and play with a _____ .

I'd drink milk from a .

I'd watch for the _____ .

Then I'd sleep on a 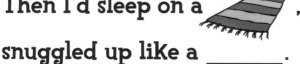 ,

snuggled up like a _____ .

Hooked on Kindergarten *Super Workbook*

A Bag Full of Rhymes

This is a game for two or more players.

How to play:

1. Copy each word in the list on the next page onto an index card. Put the cards in a paper bag.

2. The first player picks a card from the bag and says the word out loud.

3. The player thinks of a rhyming word. If he makes a rhyme, he keeps the card and gets another turn.

4. Keep taking turns until all the cards are out of the bag. The player with the most cards wins the game.

Note to Parents
If your child has trouble thinking of a rhyme, play a variation of the game by giving three word choices. For example, if your child chooses *pig*, you could say, "What rhymes with *pig*? *Big*, *bag*, or *bug*?"

98

Be a Poet

On a large sheet of paper, draw a picture of yourself.

Then choose some of the words from the list to write a poem about yourself.

fun
nice
toy
run
ice
boy
small
sweet
girl
tall
feet
curl

99

Same Size

Look at the things in each box.
Circle the two that are the same size.

What's Bigger?

Look at the pictures in each row.
Circle the one that is bigger than the other pictures.

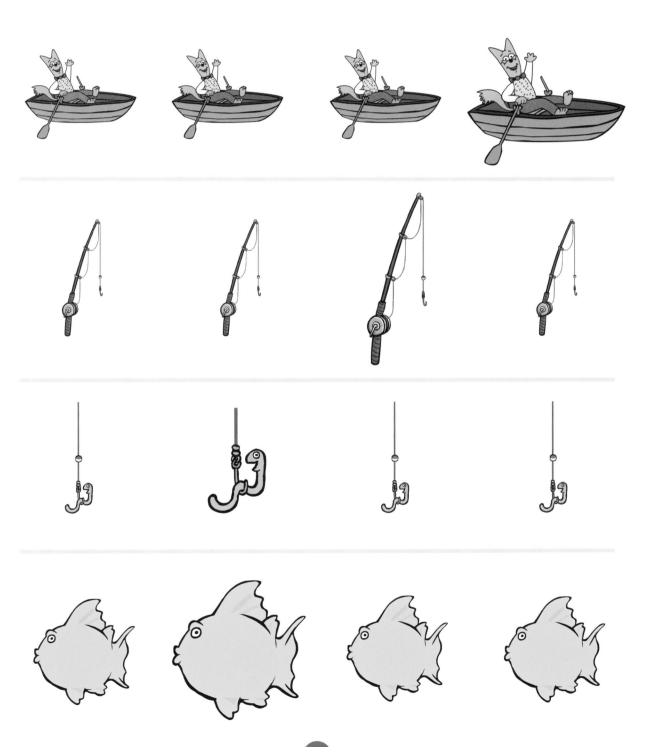

Hooked on Kindergarten *Super Workbook*

First, Next, Last

Write "1" in the square to show what happens first.
Write "2" to show what happens next.
Write "3" to show what happens last.

What's Next?

Look at the first picture in each row.
Circle a picture to show what happens next.

Hooked on Kindergarten *Super Workbook*

Two by Two

Look at the pictures in each row.
Circle the two that are the same.

A Perfect Match

Look at the pictures in each row.
Circle the two that are the same.

Hooked on Kindergarten *Super Workbook*

Perfect Pattern

Circle the picture that comes next in each pattern.

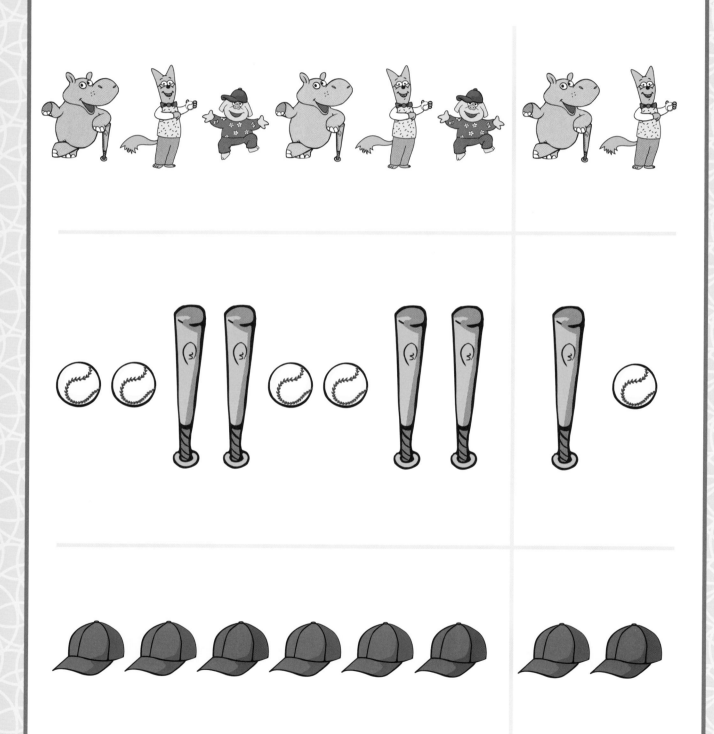

Make a Quilt

Color the shape in each row to finish the pattern.
Then make your own pattern in the last row.

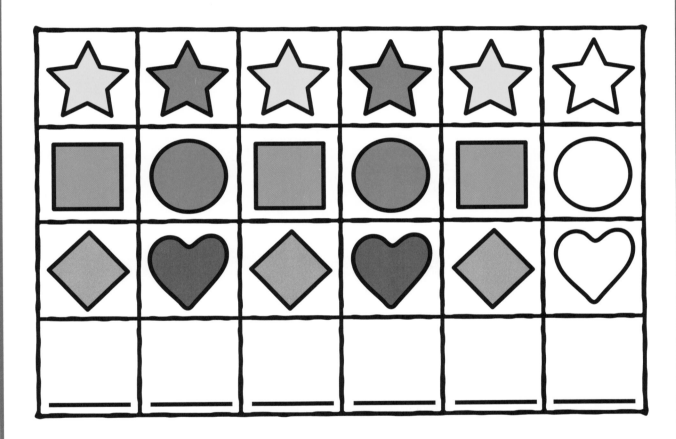

Hooked on Kindergarten *Super Workbook*

Shape Up!

Look at the things in each row.
Circle the one that matches the shape on the left.

 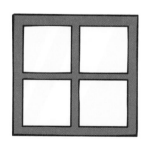  

108

Ship Shape

Use the key to color the shapes.

Key

Hooked on Kindergarten *Super Workbook*

In or Out?

Circle the ducks that are **in** Hip-O's pool.
Draw an X on the ducks that are **out** of Hip-O's pool.

Bye, Bye Birdie

Color the birds **inside** the birdhouse yellow.
Color the birds **outside** the birdhouse blue.

111

Flutter By, Butterfly

Circle the butterflies that are **over** the net.
Draw an X on the butterflies that are **under** the net.
Draw a square around the butterflies that are **next to** the net.

In the Orchard

I did it!

Color the apples **on** the table red.
Color the apples **under** the table green.
Color the apples **next to** the table yellow.

Hooked on Kindergarten *Super Workbook*

Laundry Day

Play games in the laundry room.

Try to find matching pairs of socks.

Sort pants into a row of big, bigger, biggest.

Look for clothes that are the same color.

Note to Parents
The most effective way for your child to practice basic skills is to see them applied in everyday situations. Ask your child to help you count the quarters you need at the laundromat or to sort clothes into piles of light and dark. Take turns giving clues about one item of clothing in the laundry pile, and challenge each other to find the item.

Sort the Shopping

Unpack the grocery bags.

Sort the items into groups, such as which go into the refrigerator, freezer, or cupboard.

Place cans in order by size.

Look for letters on the food packaging.

Hooked on Kindergarten *Super Workbook*

What's the Same?

Look at the pictures in each row.
Circle the two that are the same.

Hooked on Kindergarten *Super Workbook*

What's Different?

Look at the pictures in each row.
Circle the one that is different.

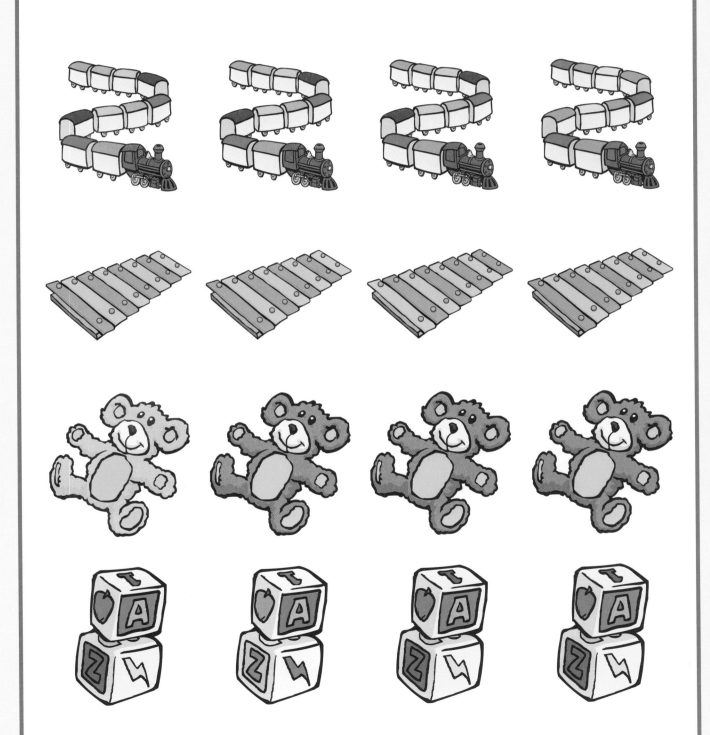

Hooked on Kindergarten *Super Workbook*

Opposites Attract

Look at the pictures on the left.
Draw a line to match each one to its opposite
on the right.

up

wet

happy

big

dry

sad

small

down

The Opposite Side

Look at the pictures in each row.
Circle the one that shows the opposite of the
first picture.

119

Hooked on Kindergarten *Super Workbook*

We Belong Together

Look at the pictures in each row.
Circle the one that belongs with the first picture.

Hooked on Kindergarten *Super Workbook*

Make the Bed

What belongs on Pig Wig's bed?
Draw lines from the bed to the things that belong on it.

121

What Does Not Belong?

Look at the pictures in each row.
Draw an X on the one that does not belong with the first picture.

Hooked on Kindergarten *Super Workbook*

Something's Wrong

Look at the pictures in each row.
Draw an X on the one that does not belong with the first picture.

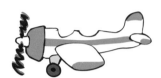  

Hooked on Kindergarten *Super Workbook*

The Perfect Pet

Which is the perfect pet for Hip-O?
Read the clues.
Then circle the pet.

Clues
1. It does not say "quack."
2. It does not eat bananas.
3. It does not have wings.

The Best Dress

Which is the best dress for Pig Wig?
Read the clues.
Then circle the dress.

Clues
1. It has polka dots.
2. It is not blue.
3. It has two buttons.

Be a Collector

Gather a collection of small scrap objects, such as feathers, buttons, fabric scraps, colored paper clips, stickers, lids from food jars, seeds, stones, seashells, leaves, or pieces of cotton.

Play games with the collection, such as placing objects in size order or using objects to create patterns.

Note to Parents
Your child can build critical thinking skills and vocabulary by playing games with the collection. Ask him to describe the way two things are alike and different. Or put a group of objects on a table and ask your child to describe them. Then, while he shuts his eyes, take away a few. Ask him to figure out which objects are missing.

My Collection

Glue things from your collection here to make a collage.

Hooked on Kindergarten *Super Workbook*

I did it!

Congratulations!

_____

_____

has successfully completed this workbook.

A Note to Hip-O

Trace the letters "T" and "I" to help Pig Wig complete her note.

To Hip-O,
I want to go to the park. Try to meet me.
It will be fun.
From Pig Wig

137

F and E

Trace, then write the letter "F."

Trace, then write the letter "E."

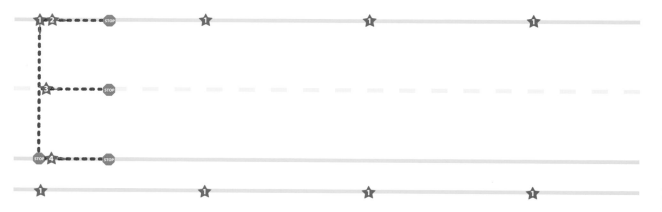

© 2006 HOP, LLC

Gift Wrap

Trace the letters "F" and "E" to complete the gift tags.

For Emma

For Ed

For Eli

For Ellen

139

L and H

Trace, then write the letter "L."

Trace, then write the letter "H."

To the Zoo!

Trace the letters "L" and "H" to complete the zoo signs.

LION

HORSE

HYENA

LEOPARD

Friendly Greetings

Trace the letters to complete the cards.

Hello to Everyone!

I Like Hip-O!

Hooked on Kindergarten *Super Workbook*

Tic-tac-toe

This is a game for two players.

What you need:
Two different-colored crayons

How to play:

1. Each player chooses one of the letters from the box below.

2. The first player writes his letter in one of the game-board squares on the opposite page.

3. The next player takes a turn.

4. Keep taking turns until one player has three of his letters in a row—up, down, or diagonally.

| T | I | F | E | L | H |

Note to Parents
Tic-tac-toe is a fun way for your child to practice handwriting skills. As your child learns to write more letters, add them to your Tic-tac-toe games.

Hooked on Kindergarten *Super Workbook*

V and W

Trace, then write the letter "V."

Trace, then write the letter "W."

Weather Report

Trace the letters "V" and "W" to complete Pop Fox's weather report.

WEATHER
WATCH

View the
Weather Vane

X and Y

Trace, then write the letter "X."

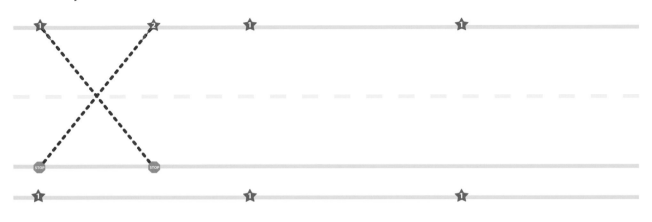

Trace, then write the letter "Y."

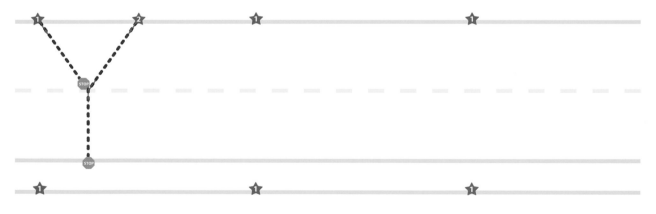

Hip-O's Playroom

Trace the letter "X" to get Hip-O to the xylophone.
Trace the letter "Y" to get Hip-O to the yo-yo.

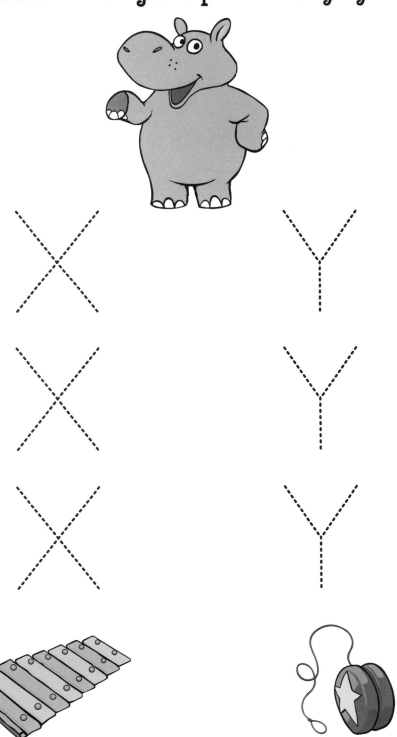

Hooked on Kindergarten *Super Workbook*

N and M

Trace, then write the letter "N."

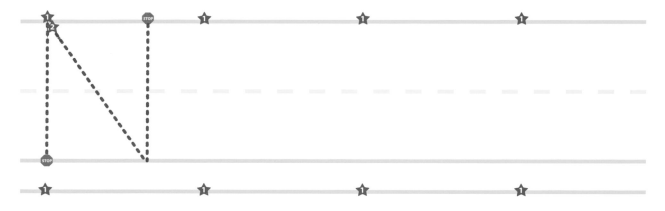

Trace, then write the letter "M."

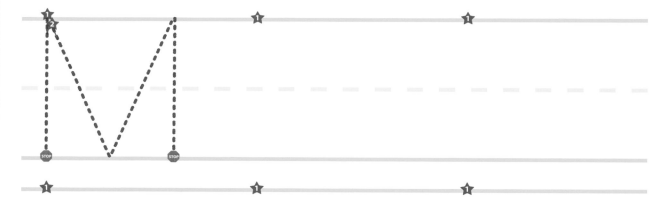

Hooked on Kindergarten *Super Workbook*

A Nice Meal

Trace the letters "N" and "M" to complete Pig Wig's menu.

MENU

Noodles

Nuts

Mushrooms

Nectarines

K, Z, and A

Trace, then write the letter "K."

Trace, then write the letter "Z."

Trace, then write the letter "A."

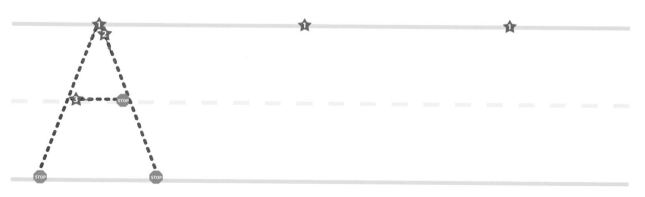

Building Blocks

Trace the letters "K," "Z," and "A" to complete Hip-O's block tower.

153

On the Road

Trace the letters to complete the postcards.

We're at the Zoo!

The Kazoo and Xylophone Music Fair

Night on the Volcano

We Went Apple Picking Yesterday!

C and O

Trace, then write the letter "C."

Trace, then write the letter "O."

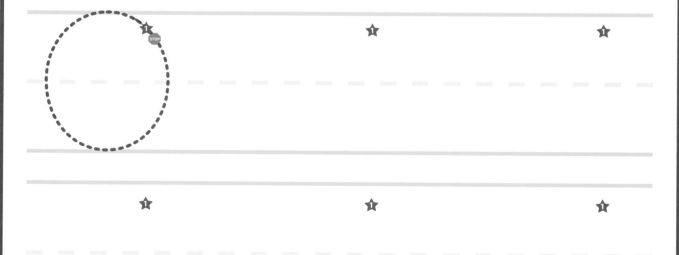

Hooked on Kindergarten *Super Workbook*

The Grocery Store

Trace the letters "C" and "O" to complete the store signs.

CARROTS

ORANGES

COOKIES

OLIVES

Hooked on Kindergarten *Super Workbook*

Q and G

Trace, then write the letter "Q."

Trace, then write the letter "G."

Secret Message

Trace the letters "Q" and "G" to complete
Dog Bug's message.

Quick!
Go to the library!
Quietly get a book.
Give it to Hip-O.

159

S and J

Trace, then write the letter "S."

Trace, then write the letter "J."

Pop Fox Shops

Trace the letters "S" and "J" to complete Pop Fox's list.

 Soup

 Jam

 Salt

 Juice

 Sunflowers

 Jellybeans

161

U and D

Trace, then write the letter "U."

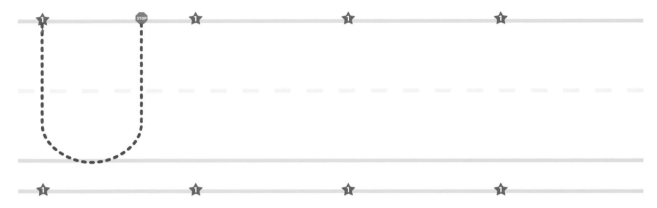

Trace, then write the letter "D."

Book Report

Trace the letters "U" and "D" to complete the book titles.

Dance with a Unicorn

Up the Dark Stairs

P, B, and R

Trace, then write the letter "P."

Trace, then write the letter "B."

Trace, then write the letter "R."

Soapbox Derby

Trace the letters "P," "B," and "R" to complete Pig Wig's car.

Pig Wig's Big Racer

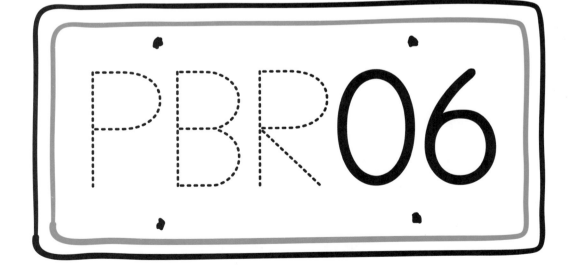

PBR06

165

The Key to It All

Trace the letters to complete Pop Fox's keyboard.

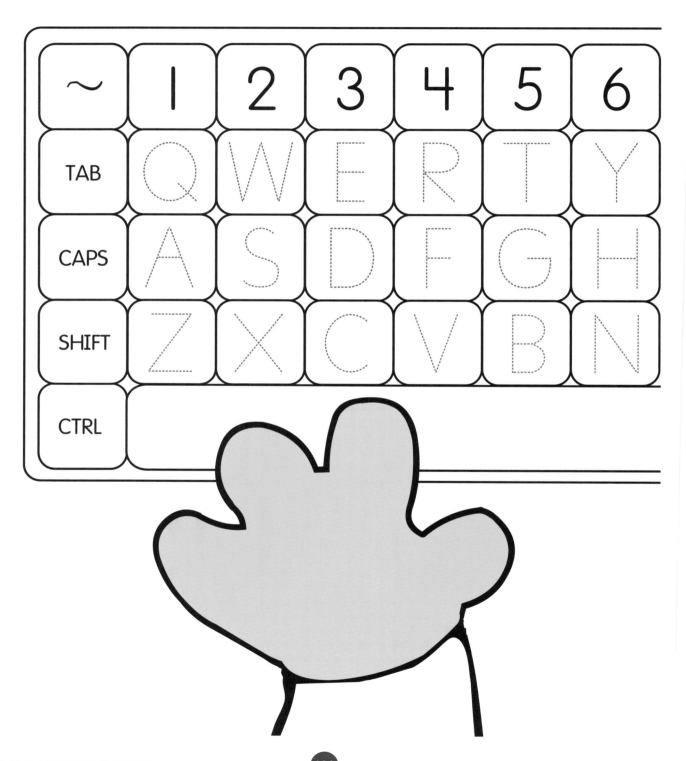

Hooked on Kindergarten *Super Workbook*

Mystery Letter

This is a game for two players.

How to play:

1. The first player chooses a letter from the box. Then he uses his finger to "write" the letter on the other player's back.

2. The other player guesses which letter the first player is writing. If the player can't guess, the first player writes it again.

3. Keep taking turns until the players have "written" all of the letters in the box.

C O Z G S J U D P B R

Note to Parents
If your child has trouble guessing a letter, give him clues about the letter, such as "This letter looks like a circle," or "This letter begins the word *rain*."

In Your Place

Make place cards for your dinner table.

Fold one index card in half for each family member.

Write the family member's name on the front half.

Then put the cards on the table to show where each person should sit.

Note to Parents
Encourage your child to practice handwriting by writing signs for your home. He might create a reminder to turn off the water while brushing teeth or a breakfast menu to post on the refrigerator.

169

l, t, and i

Trace, then write the letter "l."

Trace, then write the letter "t."

Trace, then write the letter "i."

In Our Cubbies

Trace the letters "l," "t," and "i" to complete the names on the cubbies.

Hooked on Kindergarten *Super Workbook*

j, f, and k

Trace, then write the letter "j."

Trace, then write the letter "f."

Trace, then write the letter "k."

Photo Album

Trace the letters "j," "f," and "k" to complete the captions.

I jumped rope.

I flew a kite.

I kicked a ball.

I took my jam to the fair.

v and w

Trace, then write the letter "v."

Trace, then write the letter "w."

Very Well

Trace the letter "v" to get Dog Bug to the van.
Trace the letter "w" to get Dog Bug to the wagon.

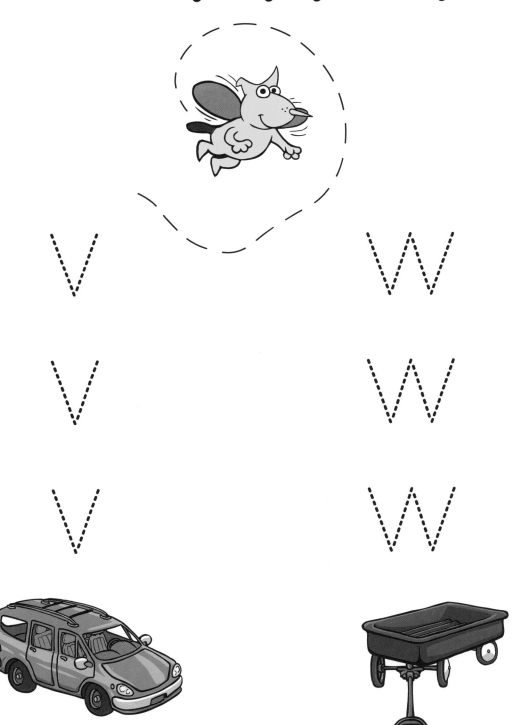

x, y, and z

Trace, then write the letter "x."

Trace, then write the letter "y."

Trace, then write the letter "z."

Tool Time

Trace the letters "h," "m," and "n" to complete the labels in Pop Fox's tool shop.

nails

helmet

net

wrench

hammer

Hooked on Kindergarten *Super Workbook*

b, p, and u

Trace, then write the letter "b."

Trace, then write the letter "p."

Trace, then write the letter "u ."

Train Tracks

Trace the letter "b" to get Pop Fox to the b train.
Trace the letter "p" to get Pig Wig to the p train.
Trace the letter "u" to get Dog Bug to the u train.

183

s, c, o, and a

Trace, then write the letter "s."

Trace, then write the letter "c."

Trace, then write the letter "o."

Trace, then write the letter "a."

Keeping Score

Trace the letters "s," "c," "o," and "a" to complete the scoreboard.

Today's Soccer Score:

Ball Hogs	2
Gray Storm	1

185

g, d, q, and e

Trace, then write the letter "g."

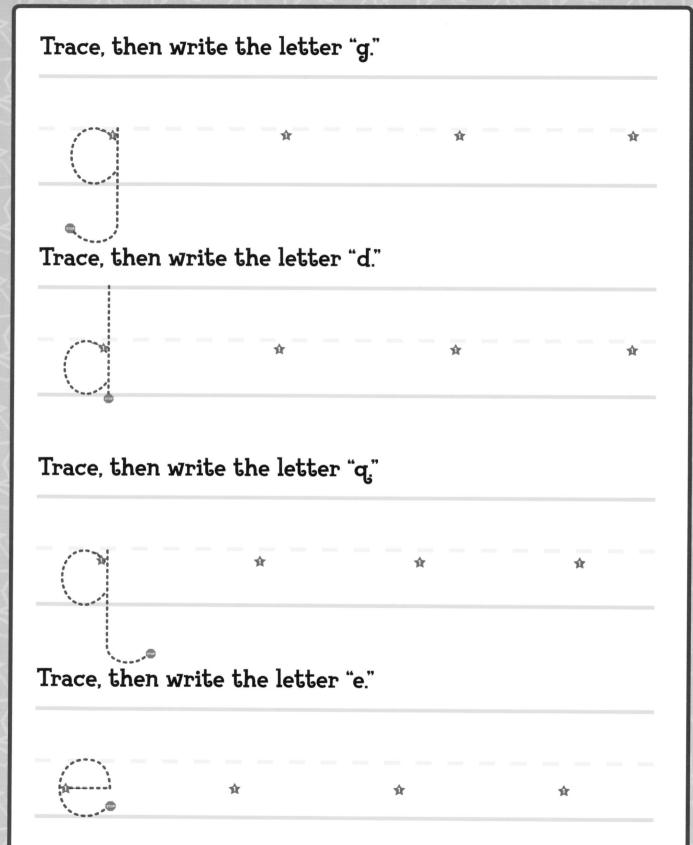

Trace, then write the letter "d."

Trace, then write the letter "q."

Trace, then write the letter "e."

Anchors Away!

Trace the letters "g," "d," "q," and "e" to complete the names of Hip-O's and Pig Wig's boats.

Aqua Marine

The Hodge Podge

From A to Z!

Trace the letters in ABC order to make a path from Hip-O to his friends.

a   m

c   b   k   l

d   j   i

e   f   g   h

You're a Writer!

Write a story.
Choose one of the story starters in the box.
Then write your story on the next page.

Note to Parents
The best handwriting practice for your child is an opportunity to write meaningfully. Ask your child to write the shopping list for you, write captions for your family photo album, or write a postcard to a friend. Keep writing materials, such as self-sticking notes and pencils, in a variety of places, such as the car or in your beachbag, so that your child can practice writing anytime.

Story Starters

Once upon a time, I met a giant…

I wished on a star and…

I found a magic wand and turned my brother into a…

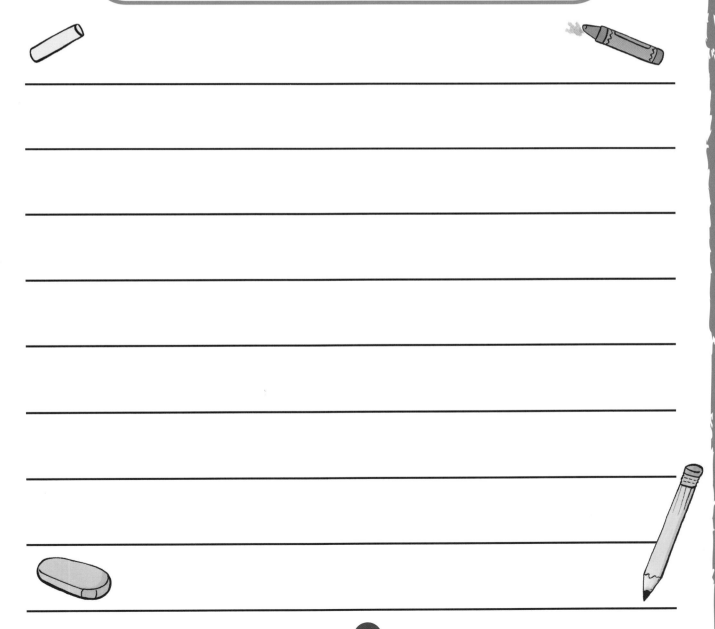

Hooked on Kindergarten *Super Workbook*

I did it!

Congratulations!

_____

_____

has successfully completed this workbook.

Kindergarten

Hooked on Math®

Math
Activities

Number Line

Follow the number line as you count
the numbers 0 to 20 out loud.

Number Blocks

Count the blocks in the stack of 10 out loud.

| 1 |
| 2 |
| 3 |
| 4 |
| 5 |
| 6 |
| 7 |
| 8 |
| 9 |
| 10 |

Count the blocks in the square of 100 out loud.

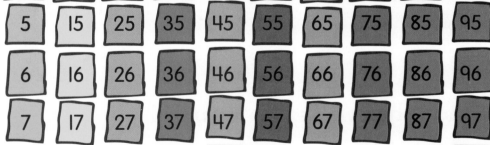

1	11	21	31	41	51	61	71	81	91
2	12	22	32	42	52	62	72	82	92
3	13	23	33	43	53	63	73	83	93
4	14	24	34	44	54	64	74	84	94
5	15	25	35	45	55	65	75	85	95
6	16	26	36	46	56	66	76	86	96
7	17	27	37	47	57	67	77	87	97
8	18	28	38	48	58	68	78	88	98
9	19	29	39	49	59	69	79	89	99
10	20	30	40	50	60	70	80	90	100

Hooked on Kindergarten *Super Workbook*

0 and 1

Trace, then write the number 0.

Trace, then write the number 1.

Space Garden

Color the pots with O flowers blue.
Color the pots with 1 flower green.

2 and 3

Trace, then write the number 2.

2 2

Trace, then write the number 3.

Pizza Party

Circle 2 things.

Circle 3 things.

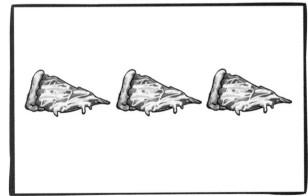

Circle 2 things.

Circle 3 things.

199

4 and 5

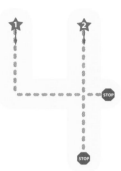

Trace, then write the number 4.

Trace, then write the number 5.

Hooked on Kindergarten *Super Workbook*

Alien Art

Draw 4 arms on the alien. Draw 5 noses on the alien.

6 and 7

Trace, then write the number 6.

6 6

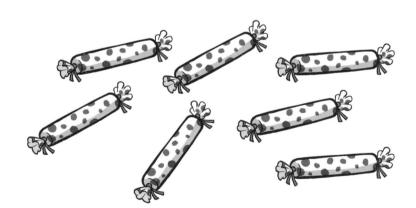

Trace, then write the number 7.

7 7

202

Space Bake

Color 6 things.

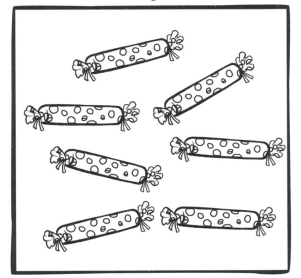

Color 7 things.

Color 6 things.

Color 7 things.

    Hooked on Kindergarten *Super Workbook*

8 and 9

Trace, then write the number 8.

Trace, then write the number 9.

Aliens Rock!

Count the things in each group.
Circle the correct answer.

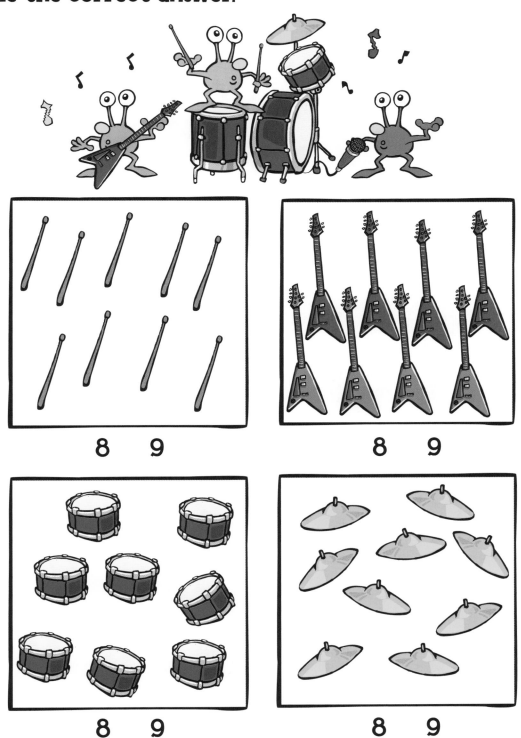

8   9   8   9

8   9   8   9

205

Eye Count

How many eyes does each alien have?
Write the number under the picture.

5 _____   _____   _____

_____   _____

_____   _____   _____

Shape Up

Draw a circle around the group of 10.
Draw a square around the group of 11.

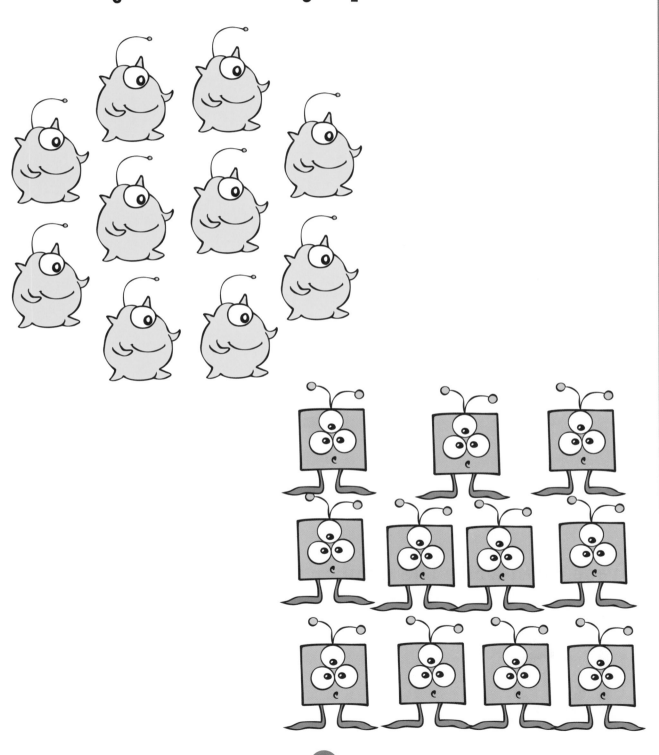

Hooked on Kindergarten *Super Workbook*

12 and 13

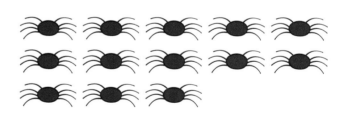

Trace, then write the number 12.

12 12

Trace, then write the number 13.

13 13

Snack Time

Count the bugs in each alien snack.
Draw a line from each snack to the alien with the matching number.

 13

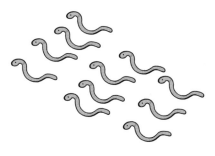

 11

 12

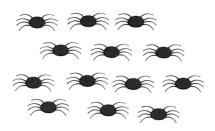

 10

14 and 15

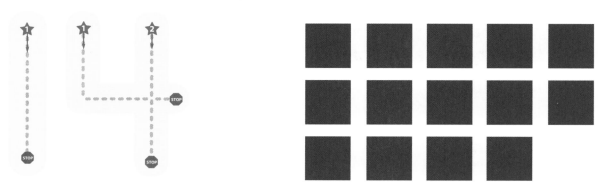

Trace, then write the number 14.

Trace, then write the number 15.

15 15

On the Blocks

Color the towers with 14 blocks red.
Color the towers with 15 blocks yellow.

© 2006 HOP, LLC

Hooked on Kindergarten *Super Workbook*

16 and 17

Trace, then write the number 16.

16 6

Trace, then write the number 17.

17

Party On!

Count the things in each group.
Circle the correct answer.

16   17

16   17

16   17

16   17

Hooked on Kindergarten *Super Workbook*

18 and 19

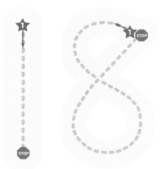

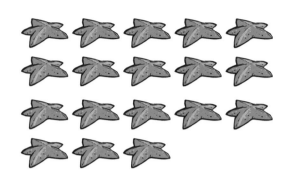

Trace, then write the number 18.

Trace, then write the number 19.

19

218

Beach Match

Trace the number on each pail.
Count the things in each group.
Draw a line from each group to the pail with
the matching number.

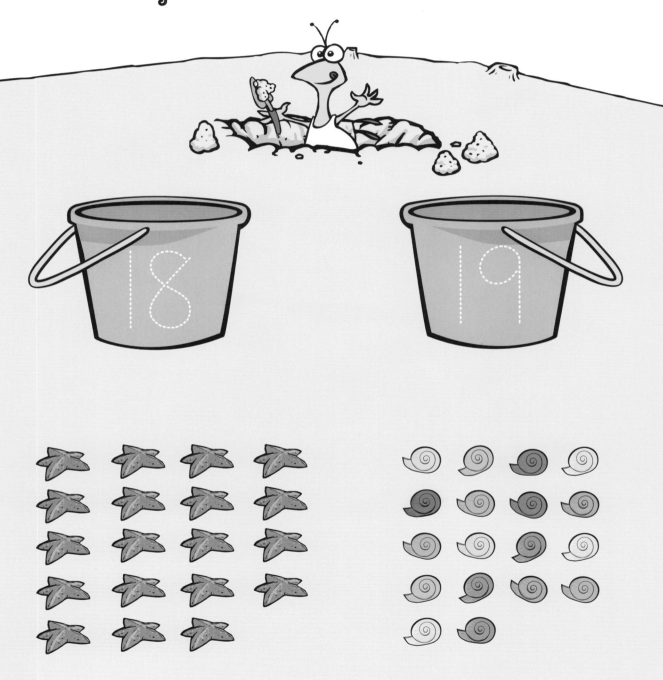

Hooked on Kindergarten *Super Workbook*

Space Train

Fill in the missing numbers.

Blastoff!

Connect the dots from 1 to 19.

Hooked on Kindergarten *Super Workbook*

Lucky 13

11 aliens. Stuck!

12 aliens. Stuck!

Hey, Harry!

13 aliens. What luck!
Unstuck!

Counting Stars

Count the stars.
Who has more?

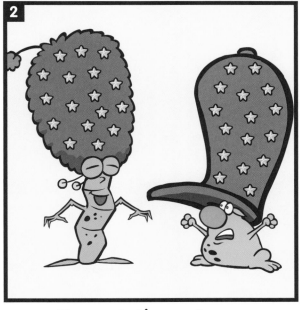

Count the stars.
Who has more now?

Count the stars.
Does anyone have more?

Count the stars.
Who has the most?

Hooked on Kindergarten *Super Workbook*

20 and 30

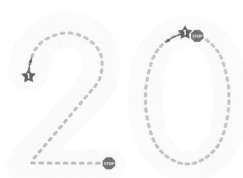 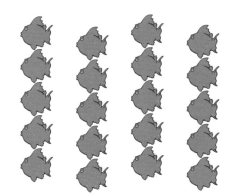

Trace, then write the number 20.

 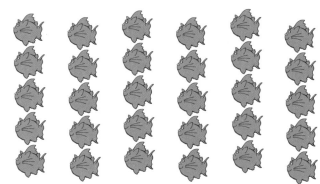

Trace, then write the number 30.

224

Go Fish

Count the fish in each group.
Circle the correct answer.

10   20   30   10   20   30

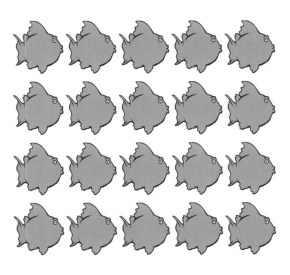
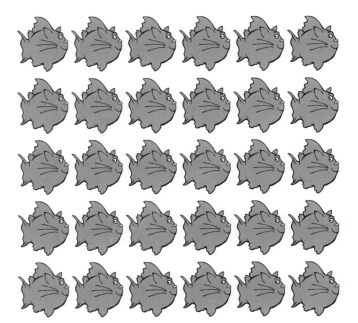

40 and 50

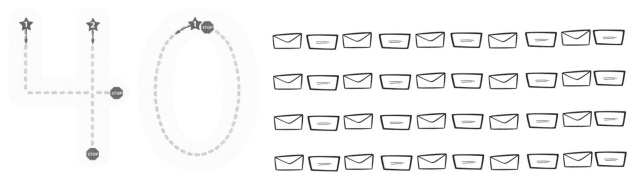

Trace, then write the number 40.

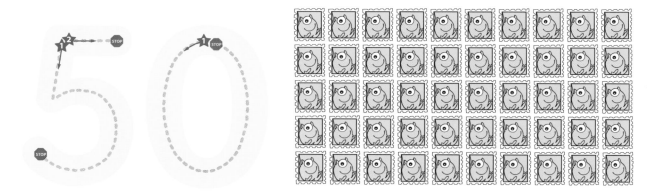

Trace, then write the number 50.

50

Hooked on Kindergarten *Super Workbook*

Special Delivery

Draw a path through the maze to get the alien to the pile of 50 letters.

60 and 70

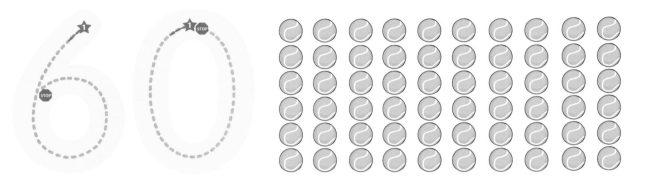

Trace, then write the number 60.

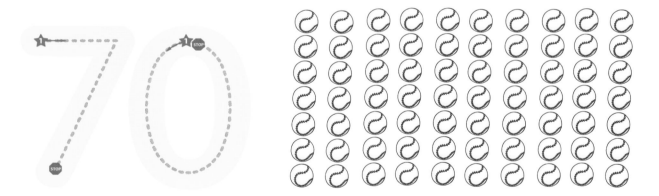

Trace, then write the number 70.

70 70

Game Time

Count the balls in each group.
Draw a line from each group to the alien
with the matching number.

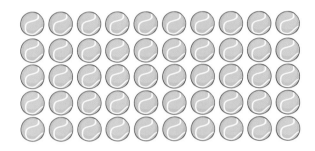

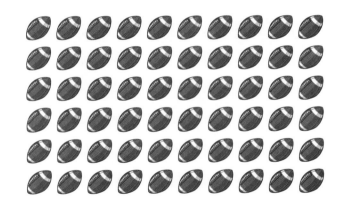

229

Moon Rocks

Count the rocks in each group.
Circle the correct answer.

20   **30**

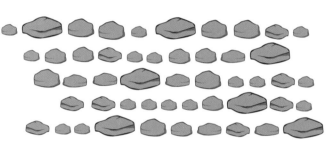

50   **60**

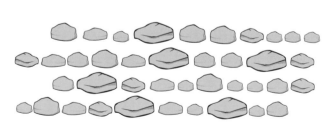

30   **40**

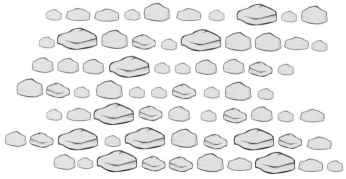

60   **70**

20   **30**

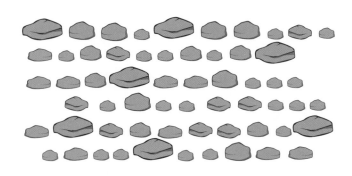

50   **60**

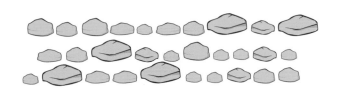

30   **40**

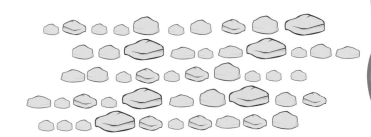

40   **50**

20   **30**

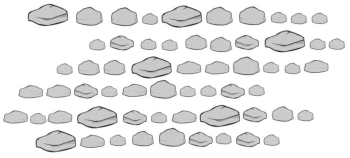

60   **70**

Hooked on Kindergarten *Super Workbook*

Scavenger Hunt

Look for the items in the chart on the next page.

When you find them, trace the number in the chart.

Note to Parents
If counting these numbers is challenging for your child, organize them into groups or rows. Introduce the idea of counting by tens, which your child will practice later in this book. If you don't have any of the items on hand, substitute something you do have, such as buttons or paper clips.

20

raisins

30

pennies

40

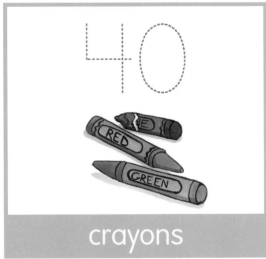

crayons

50

blocks

60

rice

70

cereal

80 and 90

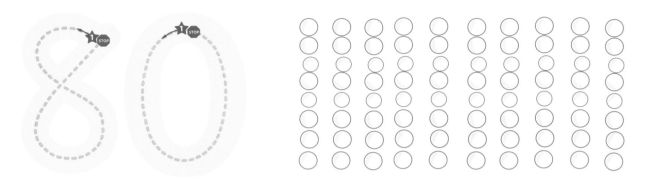

Trace, then write the number 80.

80   80

Trace, then write the number 90.

90   90

Bath Time

Count the things in each group.
Circle the correct answer.

80   90   80   90

100

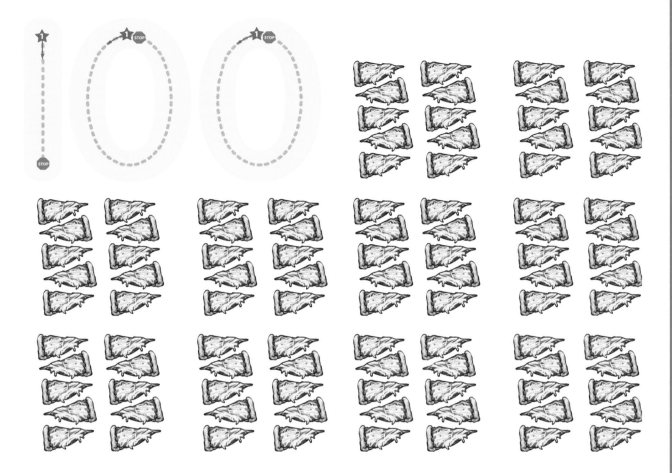

Trace, then write the number 100.

Alien Maze

Draw a path through the maze to get the hungry alien to the pile of pizza. Then count the slices of pizza. Write your answer on the line. _____

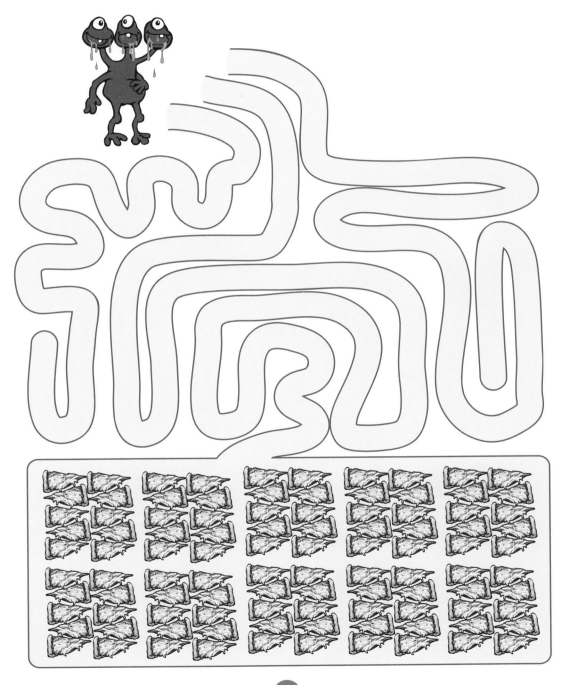

Hooked on Kindergarten *Super Workbook*

Star Match

Count the stars in each group.
Draw a line from each group to the spaceship with the matching number.

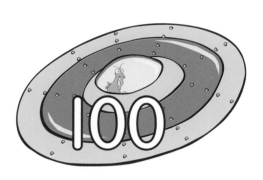

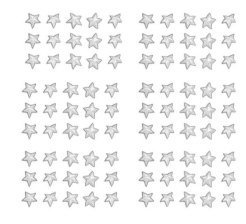

238

Color the Picture

Use the key to color the picture.

Key

50 = ███   60 = ░░░   70 = ███

80 = ███   90 = ███   100 = ███

90

60

80

50

60

70

100

80

Hooked on Kindergarten *Super Workbook*

Ribbit!

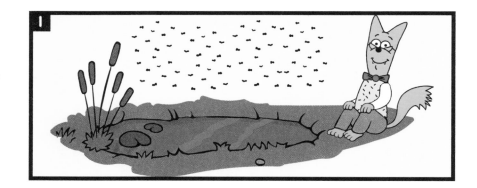

80 flies.

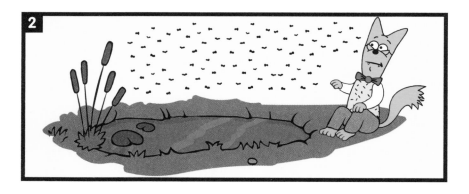

90 flies.

100 flies.

0 flies.

Turtle Race

"Go, 80!"

"Go, 90!"

"Go, 80!"
"Go, 90!"

"Go, 100!"

Hooked on Kindergarten *Super Workbook*

Counting by 2s

Count by 2s out loud. Color the numbers you say purple.

1	2
3	4
5	6
7	8
9	10
11	12
13	14
15	16
17	18
19	20

Planet Hop

Count by 2s to draw a path and get
the alien home.

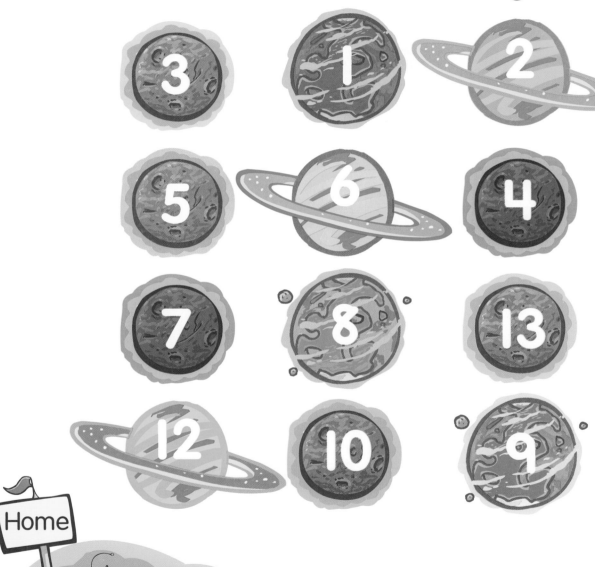

© 2006 HOP, LLC

Hooked on Kindergarten *Super Workbook*

Counting by 5s

Count by 5s out loud. Color the numbers you say orange.

1	2	3	4	5
6	7	8	9	10
11	12	13	14	15
16	17	18	19	20
21	22	23	24	25
26	27	28	29	30
31	32	33	34	35
36	37	38	39	40
41	42	43	44	45
46	47	48	49	50
51	52	53	54	55
56	57	58	59	60
61	62	63	64	65
66	67	68	69	70
71	72	73	74	75
76	77	78	79	80
81	82	83	84	85
86	87	88	89	90
91	92	93	94	95
96	97	98	99	100

High Fives

Count by 5s to fill in the missing numbers and help the alien get to his friend.

Hooked on Kindergarten *Super Workbook*

Counting by 10s

Count by 10s out loud.
Color the numbers you say green.

1	2	3	4	5	6	7	8	9	10
11	12	13	14	15	16	17	18	19	20
21	22	23	24	25	26	27	28	29	30
31	32	33	34	35	36	37	38	39	40
41	42	43	44	45	46	47	48	49	50
51	52	53	54	55	56	57	58	59	60
61	62	63	64	65	66	67	68	69	70
71	72	73	74	75	76	77	78	79	80
81	82	83	84	85	86	87	88	89	90
91	92	93	94	95	96	97	98	99	100

On Thin Ice

Connect the dots by 10s from 10 to 100 to help the alien score his goal.

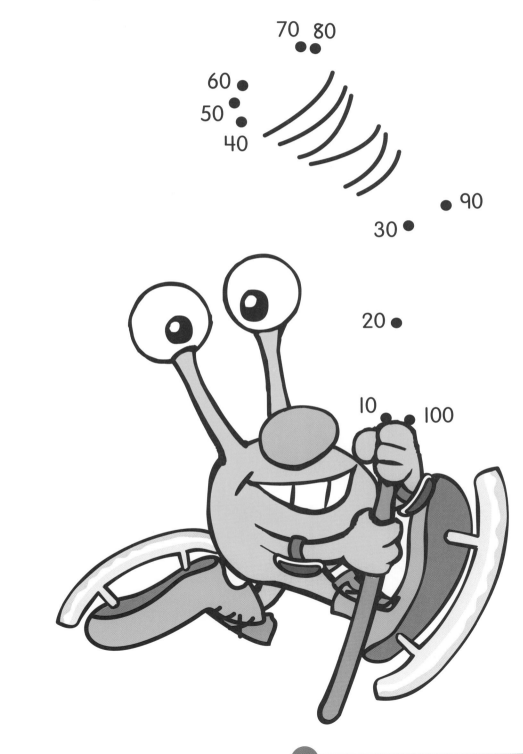

© 2006 HOP, LLC

Hooked on Kindergarten *Super Workbook*

Before

1 comes **before** 2.

Fill in the number that comes **before**.

___ 3 4

___ 7 8

___ 10 11

___ 18 19

After

3 comes after 2.

Fill in the number that comes after.

4 5 ___

8 9 ___

10 11 ___

18 19 ___

Hooked on Kindergarten *Super Workbook*

Between

2 is **between** 1 and 3.

Fill in the number that comes **between**.

3 _____ 5

6 _____ 8

17 _____ 19

More, Please

Fill in the number that comes **before**.

_____   2   3

_____   16   17

Fill in the number that comes **after**.

7   8   _____

11   12   _____

Fill in the number that comes **between**.

7   _____   9

18   _____   20

   Hooked on Kindergarten *Super Workbook*

Out of This World

These planets are lined up to count by 10s.
One number is missing in each row.
Fill in the missing number.

40   _____   60

10   20   _____

80   90   _____

_____   30   40

2, 4, 6, 8!

Count the shoes by 2s.
Circle the number that should come next.

 2    4

8   6

 2    4    6    8

10   12

 2    4   6   8   10

12   20

 2    4   6

10   8

Hooked on Kindergarten *Super Workbook*

Counting Game

Copy and color the cards on the next page onto index cards.

Separate the yellow and red cards into two piles.

Mix up the cards in each pile. Pick one card from each pile.

How high can you count?

Note to Parents
You can use the cards to review with your child counting to 100 and counting by 2s, 5s, and 10s. All are important math skills that your child needs to master and that will lead to greater understanding of more sophisticated math skills, such as multiplication and division. If your child has trouble following the directions, count along with him.

count by 2s	count by 2s	count by 5s	count by 5s
count by 10s	count by 10s	count from 0-10	count from 0-10
count from 10-20	count from 10-20	count from 50-100	count from 50-100

Hooked on Kindergarten *Super Workbook*

I did it!

Congratulations!

_____

- - - - - - - - - - - - - - - - - - - -

_____

has successfully completed this workbook.

Kindergarten
Hooked on Learning®
Puzzles and Mazes

The Rainy Day

Connect the dots from A to Z to help Pig Wig get out of the rain.

Hooked on Kindergarten *Super Workbook*

Stripes Are Nice

Use the Key to color the umbrellas.

Key
1 =   2 =   3 =   4 =

259

Get Dressed

Draw a path through the maze to get Pig Wig to her raincoat and hat. Hurry or she'll get wet!

Puddle Fun

Who likes to stomp in puddles with Pig Wig?
Connect the dots from 1 to 40 to find out.

Match Game

Circle the two boots that are exactly the same.

262

A Rainy Maze

Draw a path from raindrop to raindrop to help Hip-O get to Pig Wig's house.

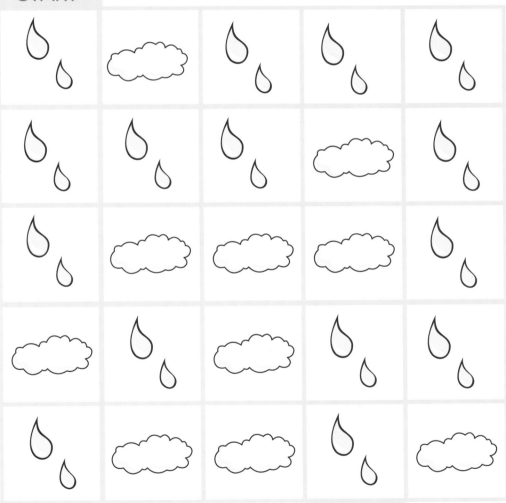

START

Hooked on Kindergarten *Super Workbook*

Finish Hip-O and Pig Wig's puzzle.
Circle the correct piece.

Hooked on Kindergarten *Super Workbook*

Where will Hip-O and Pig Wig go on their pretend journey?

Say the name of each thing out loud.

Write the first letter of each thing's name on the line below it.

_____ _____ _____

_____   _____   _____   _____   _____

    Hooked on Kindergarten *Super Workbook*

Rainy-Day Music

The next time it rains, make some music!

Use the directions on the next page to make your own musical instruments.

Then tap, clap, or sing a song.

Before you know it, the sun will come out again!

Note to Parents
If you don't have the materials to make instruments, you can still have musical fun on a rainy day. Turn up the radio and have a dance party. Make up new dances with funny names, like "The Frog" or "The Slime."

Simple Shaker

You will need:

An empty jar with a lid
Dried beans, rice, or round cereal pieces

Fill the jar with beans or other small items. Close the lid tightly, then shake!

Quick Kazoo

You will need:

A paper-towel tube   Waxed paper
A rubber band

Punch a small hole near one end of the paper-towel tube. Cover that end with waxed paper and secure with a rubber band. Put your mouth by the open end and hum.

Rain Stick

You will need:

A paper-towel tube   Toothpicks   Dried beans
Rubber bands   Paper

Poke several toothpicks through the tube in different places. Cover one end of the tube with paper and secure with a rubber band. Put a big handful of dried beans in the tube. Cover the open end with paper and secure with a rubber band. Then gently move the tube back and forth to make the sound of rain as the beans travel over the toothpicks.

Hooked on Kindergarten *Super Workbook*

Circle the words that rhyme with **fin** in the puzzle. Look across and down.

bin	pin	thin	tin	win

t	h	i	n	b	i
t	i	n	w	i	n
n	t	p	i	n	w

Hip-O is ready to swim, too!
Draw a path through the maze.

Start

Finish

Sand Art

Hip-O and Pig Wig are building things in the sand. What will they build? Is it a castle? A shark? A tower? Use crayons to draw a picture of it!

Draw a Fish

Hip-O has found a fish!
Using a pencil and eraser, follow steps 1 to 4 to draw a fish.

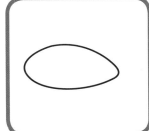

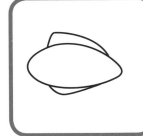

1. Draw the body shape.

2. Add top and bottom fins.

3. Add the tail fin.

4. Erase some lines, and add an eye.

Hooked on Kindergarten *Super Workbook*

Crab Chase

Pig Wig has found a crabby crab!
Draw a path through the maze to help Pig Wig get back
to her umbrella.

272

On the Beach

These pictures of Hip-O look the same, but they are different in 6 places.
Can you circle all of the things that are different?

273

Shell Search

Pig Wig is searching for seashells.
Can you find 10 shells hidden in this picture?

Too Hot!

Pig Wig and Hip-O are thinking of something that will cool them off.
Say the name of each thing out loud.
Write the first letter of each thing's name on the line below it.

_____   _____   _____   _____

Hooked on Kindergarten *Super Workbook*

Anywhere Games

You can play these games anywhere—on the beach, in a car, or while waiting in line at the supermarket.

You don't need any special items.

So what are you waiting for? It's game time!

Letter Search

Each player must find the letters of the alphabet in order. Look on signs, cars, buildings—even on clothing people are wearing. When you spot a letter, call it out! Whoever calls out the letters A to Z first is the winner.

Animal Alphabet

The object of this game is to think of the name of an animal that starts with each letter of the alphabet. The first player names an animal that begins with "a." Then the next player names an animal that begins with "b." If one player gets stuck, he can pass the letter to the next player. Keep going until one player gets to "z." Play this game with the names of people, food, or cartoon characters.

Count to 10

In this game, each player gets to shout out the name of something to count. In a car or a bus, a player might say, "Count 10 stop signs!" Then each player must look for 10 stop signs and count them out loud as he sees them. Keep naming things to count. On a beach, count 10 boogie boards, 10 blue bathing suits, 10 balls, 10 towels, or 10 seagulls.

Snow Good!

Hip-O and Pig Wig like playing in the snow.
Circle everything you see in this picture that begins
with the letter "s."

On Thin Ice

Use your finger to follow the tangled laces.
Which skates belong together?
Write your answers on the lines below.

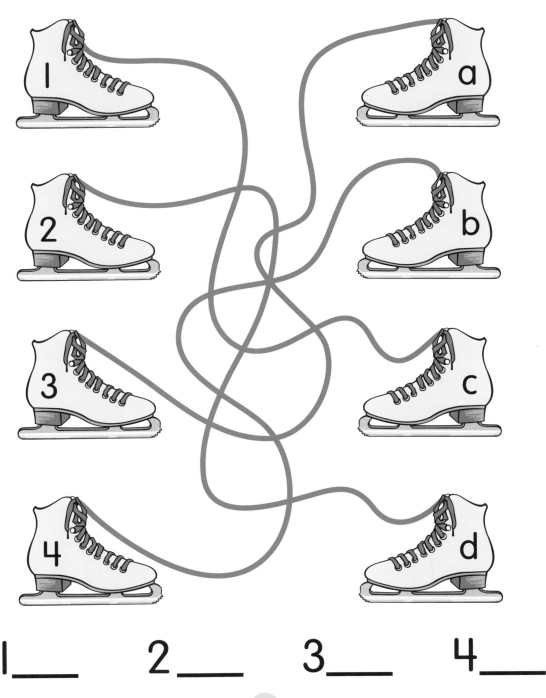

1____   2____   3____   4____

Hooked on Kindergarten *Super Workbook*

A Great Skate!

Draw a path through the letters to spell out "ice skate" so Hip-O can cross the pond and get some hot chocolate.

i	c	e	s	u
z	e	v	g	p
h	s	k	a	t
f	k	j	t	x
n	r	q	e	m

Finish

A Frosty Friend

Help Pig Wig finish her snowman.
Draw a face and arms, then give the snowman a hat,
scarf, buttons, or whatever you want!

Hooked on Kindergarten *Super Workbook*

Down the Hill

How will Pig Wig get down the hill?
Connect the dots from 1 to 30 to find out.

282

Can you circle the penguin that is different?

Hooked on Kindergarten *Super Workbook*

Let It Snow

Can you find these three pictures in a row?
Look up, down, and across.
Circle the three when you find them.

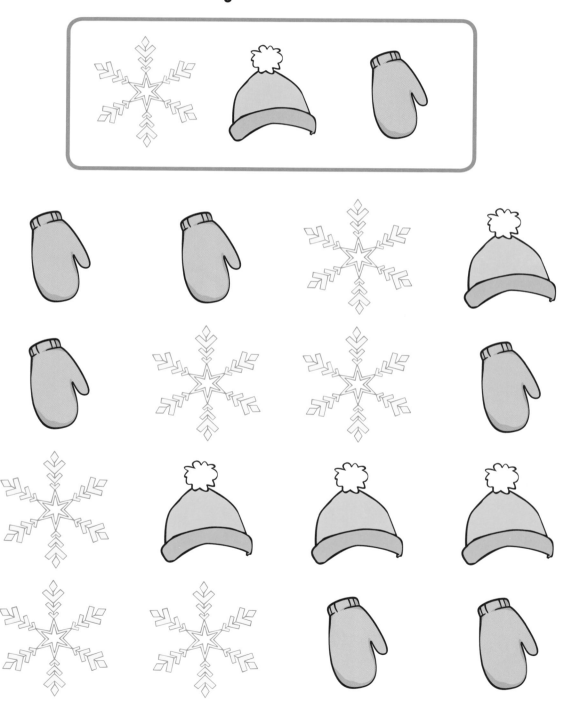

Let's Pretend

Hip-O and Pig Wig want to pretend they are somewhere with a lot of animals.
Say the name of each thing out loud.
Write the first letter of each thing's name on the line below it.

_____   _____   _____   _____   _____

    Hooked on Kindergarten *Super Workbook*

Silly Snowman

This is a game for two players.

You will need:

A die

A pencil or crayon

How to play:

1. The first player rolls the die. He writes the number on the die next to the first word on the list on the next page. Then he draws that many eyes on his snowman.

2. Players take turns rolling the die for each part of the snowman.

3. Continue until the lists are complete.

Note to Parents
You may photocopy the blank snowmen on the next page so that you can play the "Silly Snowman" game again and again. If you play with your child, use your finished snowmen to practice basic math skills. Compare the number of eyes, noses, and so on. Ask questions such as "Does your snowman have more eyes than mine?" "Do they have the same amount?" "How many more arms does my snowman have?"

eyes _____

noses _____

arms _____

hats_____

buttons_____

eyes _____

noses _____

arms _____

hats_____

buttons_____

Animals on the Farm

What animals will Pig Wig and Hip-O see on the farm?
Circle all the farm animals you see.

Rhyme Time

Look at the pictures in each row.
Say their names out loud.
Circle the thing whose name rhymes with the name
of the animal on the left.

Hooked on Kindergarten *Super Workbook*

The Chicken Coop

Pig Wig is feeding the chickens.
Using a pencil and eraser, follow steps 1 to 4 to
draw a chicken.

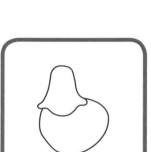

1. Draw shapes
   for the head
   and body.

2. Draw wings
   and a tail.

3. Draw feet.

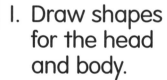

4. Draw eyes,
   a beak, and
   a comb.

Hide and Seek

Where is Hip-O hiding?
Connect the dots from 1 to 25 to find out.

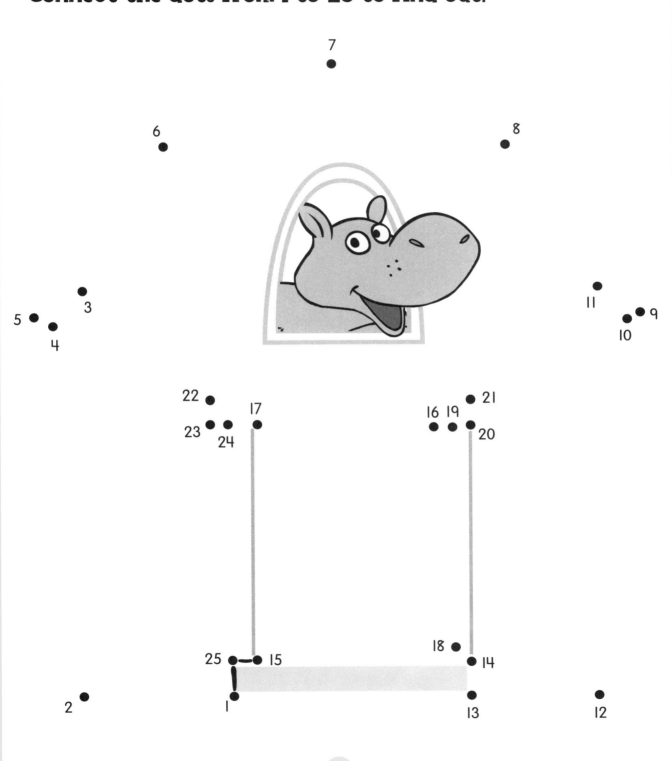

Tractor Time

Draw a path through the maze to help Pig Wig find her way out of the cornfield.

Carrots and Corn

Draw a path through the carrots and corn to get from start to finish.

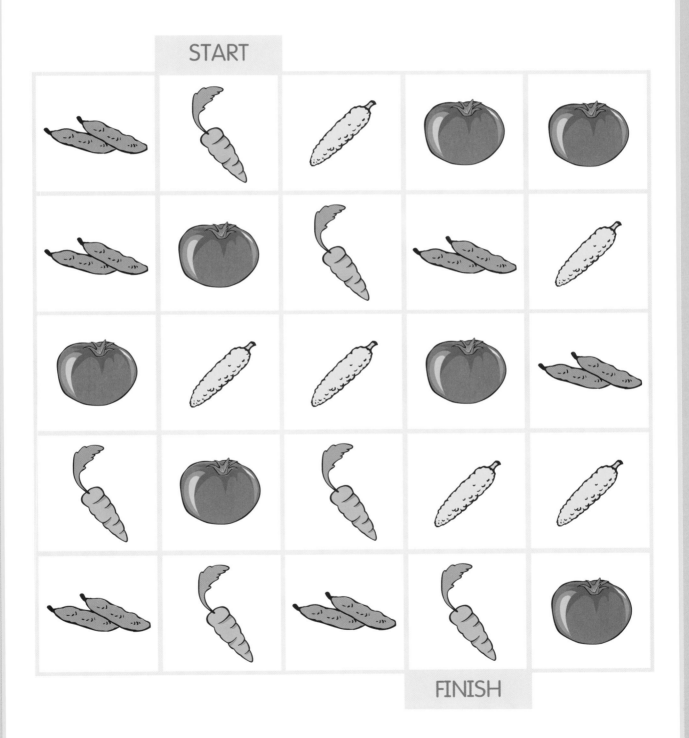

Hooked on Kindergarten *Super Workbook*

Yummy Shapes

How many of each shape can you find on the table? Write your answers on the lines.

◯ _____   △ _____

Hooked on Kindergarten *Super Workbook*

Pig Wig and Hip-O are hungry. What will they eat?
Say the name of each thing out loud.
Write the first letter of each thing's name on the line below it.

_____   _____   _____   _____   _____

Hooked on Kindergarten *Super Workbook*

Stop to Shop

Pig Wig and Hip-O are shopping for food.
Draw a path through the maze to see who will get
to the cash register.

Hooked on Kindergarten *Super Workbook*

Food Hunt

Circle the food words hidden in the puzzle.
Look across and down.

apples 🍎 bread 🍞 cheese 🧀 eggs 🥚

grapes 🍇 milk 🥛 juice 🧃

c	h	e	e	s	e
a	p	p	l	e	s
e	b	r	e	a	d
g	m	i	l	k	a
g	r	a	p	e	s
s	j	u	i	c	e

Hooked on Kindergarten *Super Workbook*

Pizza Party

Pig Wig made a pizza.
Circle the picture that is different in each row.

Yum Yum!

Use the Key to color the picture.

Key

1 = [ ]   2 = [ ]   3 = [ ]

Hooked on Kindergarten *Super Workbook*

Pasta Tangle

Pig Wig and Hip-O like pasta, too.
Which bowl of pasta belongs to each friend?
Use your finger to follow the tangled pasta.
Write your answers on the lines below.

Pig Wig _____

Hip-O _____

A Pretty Plate

Pig Wig loves pizza.
What is your favorite food?
Draw your favorite thing to eat on the plate.

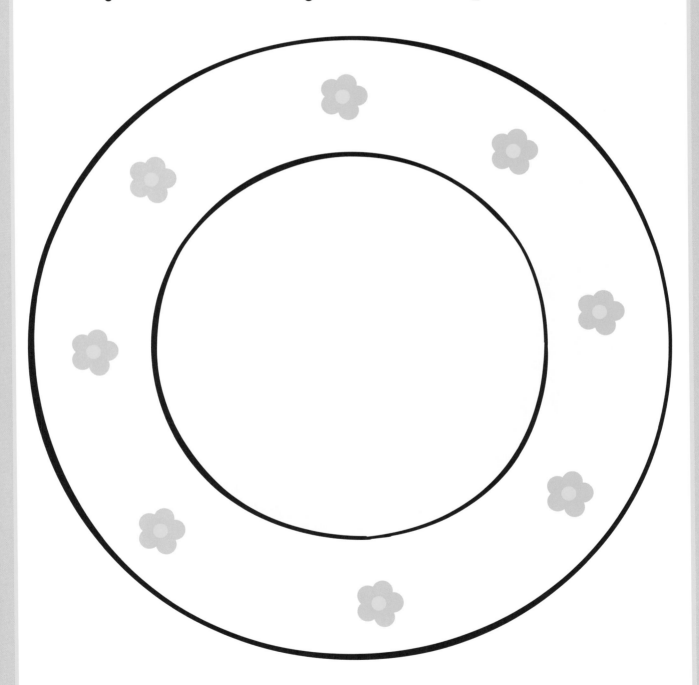

Hooked on Kindergarten *Super Workbook*

What Comes Next?

Circle the picture that comes next in each pattern.

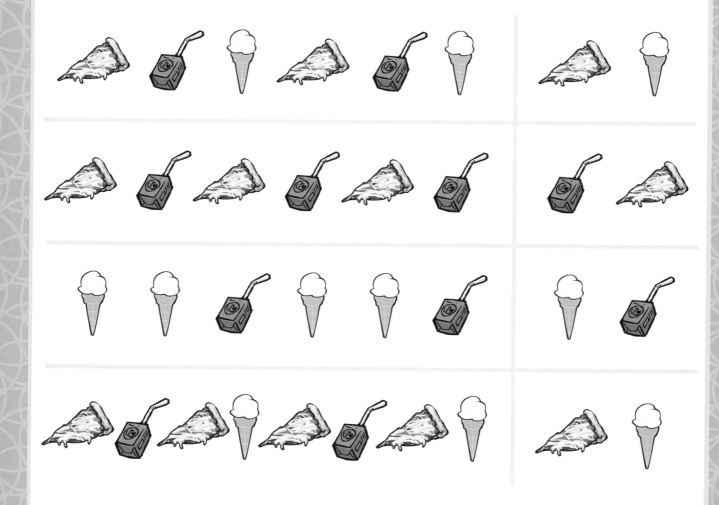

Who will Pig Wig and Hip-O pretend to meet now?
Say the name of each thing out loud.
Write the first letter of each thing's name on the line below it.

_____   _____   _____   _____   _____

Hooked on Kindergarten *Super Workbook*

Lost in the Castle

Pig Wig and Hip-O want to see the queen of the castle. Draw a path through the castle to help them find the queen.

The Perfect Plan

Use the pictures to help you read the story.

Once upon a time there was a . She lived

in a . The had a beautiful .

A lived near the . The liked .

He flew to the and took the .

The was sad. She called on and for

help. The asked them to go to the and get

back the .

 and had a plan.

They knew how to get the back.

 packed a  .

 said, "Let's go!"

And that is just what they did!

Hooked on Kindergarten *Super Workbook*

Colors in the Crown

What color is each gem?
Use the picture clues and the word box to fill in the puzzle.

blue =	yellow =	orange =
green =	red =	

Across:

1. 

5. 

Down:

2. 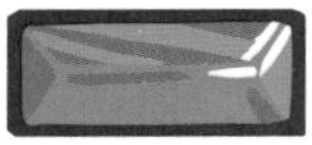

3. 

4. 

The Dragon's Den

Draw a path through the triangle-shaped jewels to help Pig Wig and Hip-O get to the dragon's den.

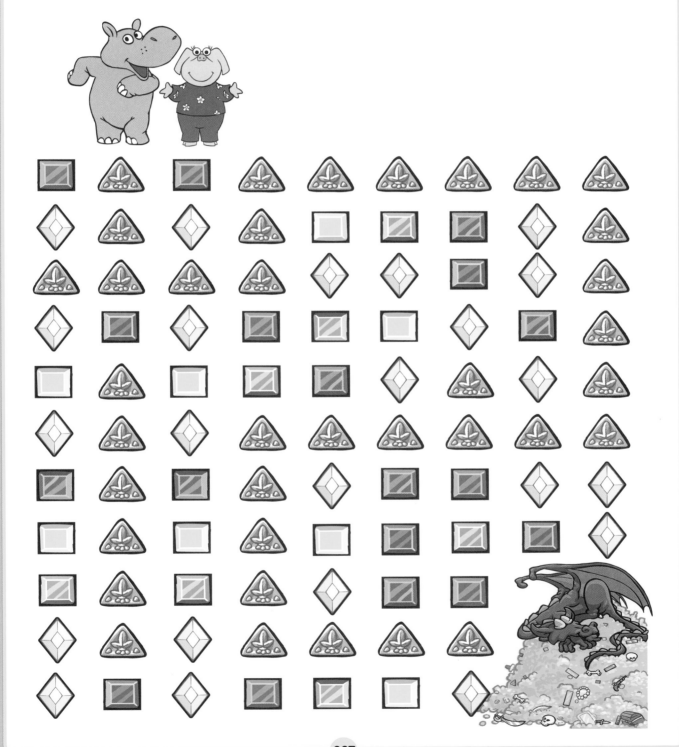

Hooked on Kindergarten *Super Workbook*

Hidden Treasures

Can you find 11 crowns hidden in this picture?

Pig Wig and Hip-O want to make a trade with the
dragon to get the crown.
Connect the dots from 1 to 20
to see what they brought to trade.

5
1
6
4
11
20
10
2
19
7
18
17
3
16
13
14
15
12
8
9

Color the Crown

The queen's crown is safe!
Use the Key to color the jewels in the crown.

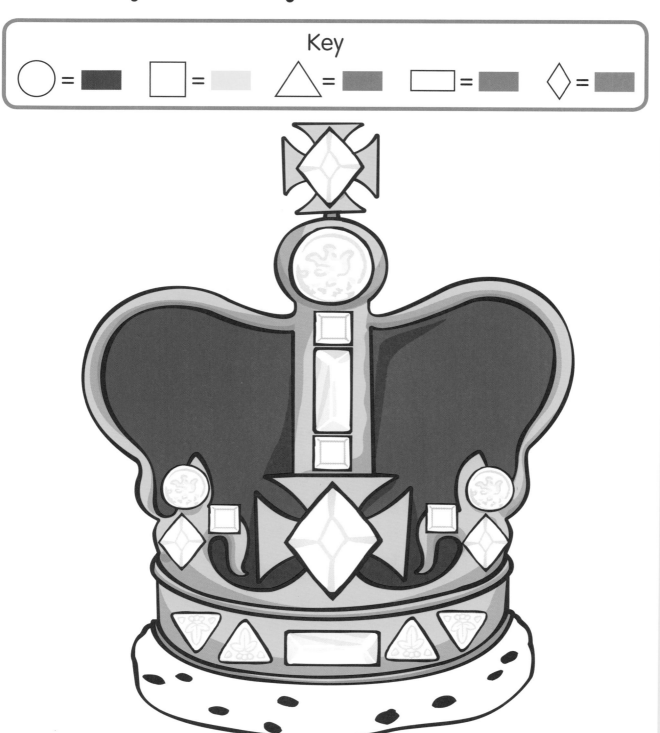

Hooked on Kindergarten *Super Workbook*

Different Dragons

I did it!

These two dragons look the same, but they are different in 6 places.
Can you circle all of the things that are different?

Hooked on Kindergarten *Super Workbook*

Play Pretend

Hip-O and Pig Wig have fun playing pretend.

You can play pretend, too.

Write the names of the places in the box on index cards.

Place the cards face down. Pick a card.

Then pretend you are in that place.

What happens on your pretend adventure?

Draw a picture of it on the next page.

> in the rain
>
> in the snow
>
> in a castle
>
> on the beach
>
> on a farm
>
> in a restaurant

Note to Parents
You can make cards with additional places, such as the moon, a mountain, a big city, and so on. Take the activity further by writing a story with your child about his pretend adventure.

Hooked on Kindergarten *Super Workbook*

Hello, Sun!

Can you find these three pictures in a row?
Look up, down, and across.
Circle the three when you find them.

To the Park!

Draw a letter "p" path to get Pig Wig and Hip-O to the park.

p	a	o	b	e	h
p	m	p	p	p	k
p	p	p	n	p	u
v	x	s	r	p	t
z	b	a	h	p	p
n	c	y	d	c	p

Hooked on Kindergarten *Super Workbook*

My Shadow

Draw a line from each picture of Pig Wig to the matching shadow.

Hat Hunt

Look at the hats on the page.
Circle the ones you have seen in this book.
Go back and look if you have to!

Hooked on Kindergarten *Super Workbook*

Answer Key

PAGE 258

PAGE 259

PAGE 260

PAGE 261
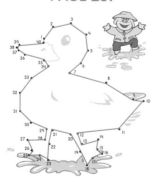

PAGE 262

PAGE 263
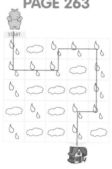

PAGE 264

PAGE 265
the beach

PAGE 268

PAGE 269

PAGE 272

PAGE 273

PAGE 274
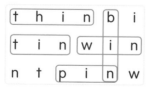

PAGE 275
snow

PAGE 278
sun, sled, snowman
scarf, sticks, shovel

PAGE 279
1-c; 2-d;
3-a; 4-b

PAGE 280

PAGE 282

PAGE 283

PAGE 284
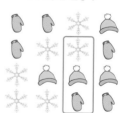

PAGE 285
a farm

PAGE 288
cow, chicken, horse,
pig, sheep, goat

318

PAGE 289
hen/pen; pig/wig;
ox/box; cat/hat

PAGE 291
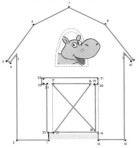

PAGE 292

PAGE 293
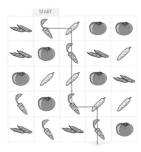

PAGE 294
14 circles, 5 triangles

PAGE 295
pizza

PAGE 296
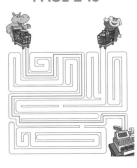

PAGE 297

PAGE 298

PAGE 299

PAGE 300
Pig Wig: 1
Hip-O: 2

PAGE 302

PAGE 303
queen

PAGE 304

PAGE 306
Across:
1. orange
5. yellow
Down:
2. red
3. green
4. blue

PAGE 307
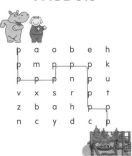

PAGE 308

PAGE 309

PAGE 310

PAGE 311

PAGE 314

PAGE 315

PAGE 316

PAGE 317

319

I did it!

Congratulations!

_____

_____

has successfully completed this workbook.